A VISUAL HISTORY OF THE WORLD

A VISUAL HISTORY OF THE GREAT CIVILIZATIONS

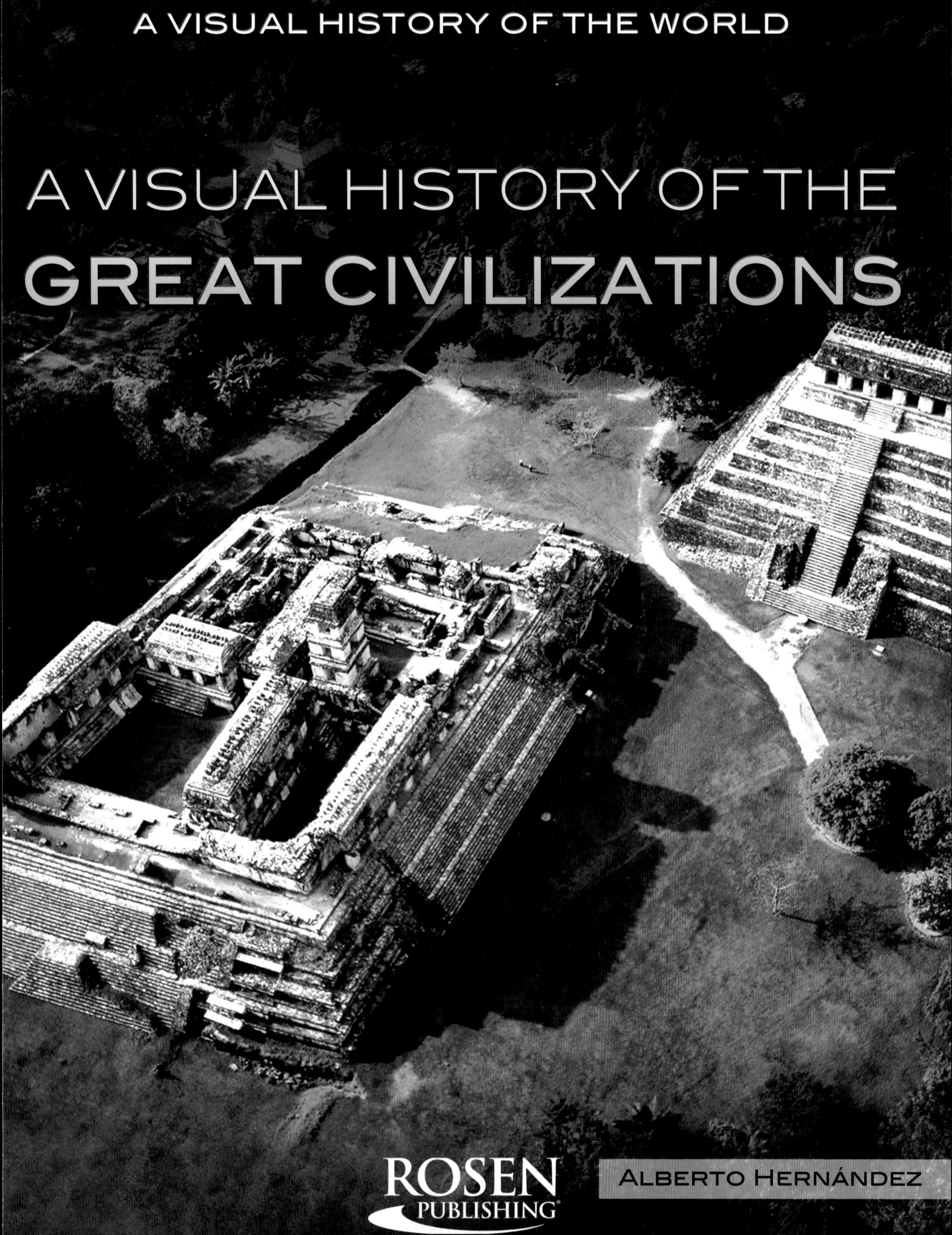

ROSEN PUBLISHING

ALBERTO HERNÁNDEZ

This edition published in 2017 by
The Rosen Publishing Group, Inc.
29 East 21st Street
New York, NY 10010

Library of Congress Cataloging-in-Publication Data

Names: Hernández, Alberto, author.
Title: A visual history of the great civilizations / Alberto Hernández
Description: New York : Rosen Publishing, 2017. | Series: A visual history of the world | Audience: Grades 7 to 12. | Includes bibliographical references
and index..
Identifiers: LCCN 2016035132 | ISBN 9781499465747 (library bound)
Subjects: LCSH: Civilization—History—Juvenile literature. | Civilization—History—Pictorial works—Juvenile literature.
Classification: LCC CB69.2 .F38 2017 | DDC 909—dc23
LC record available at https://lccn.loc.gov/2016035132

Manufactured in Malaysia

Metric Conversion Chart
1 inch = 2.54 centimeters; 25.4 millimeters
1 foot = 30.48 centimeters
1 yard = .914 meters
1 square foot = .093 square meters
1 square mile = 2.59 square kilometers
1 ton = .907 metric tons
1 pound = 454 grams
1 mile = 1.609 kilometers
1 cup = 250 milliliters
1 ounce = 28 grams
1 fluid ounce = 30 milliliters
1 teaspoon = 5 milliliters
1 tablespoon = 15 milliliters
1 quart = .946 liters
355 degrees F = 180 degrees Celsius

Original Idea Nuria Cicero
Editorial Coordination Alberto Hernández
Editorial Team Alberto Moreno de la Fuente, Luciana Rosende, Virginia Iris Fernández, Pablo Pineau, Matías Loewy, Joan Soriano, Mar Valls, Leandro Jema
Proofreaders Marta Kordon, Edgardo D'Elio
Design María Eugenia Hiriart
Layout Laura Ocampo, Clara Miralles, Paola Fornasaro

Photography Age Fotostock, Getty Images, Science Photo Library, National Geographic, Latinstock, Album, ACI, Cordon Press
Illustrations and Infographics Trexel Animation, Trebol Animation,
WOW Studio, Sebastián Giacobino, Néstor Taylor, Nuts Studio, Steady in Lab, 3DN, Federico Combi, Pablo Aschei, Leonardo César, 4D News, Rise Studio, Ariel Roldán, Dorian Vandegrift, Zoom Desarrollo Digitales, Marcelo Regalado.

Contents

Introduction

It was not until just over 12,000 years ago that humanity began to abandon the long period known as Prehistory. With its sedentary **lifestyle** and the technological revolution, the Neolithic Era laid the foundations for the emergence of the primitive agriculture, the agricultural surplus and increasingly complex social organization models. It was in this context that the human being entered a new evolution cycle: the stage of civilization or **High Cultures**.

The first Civilizations appeared in the late fourth millennium BC, in the geographic areas where the environment provided better chances of survival to its inhabitants, usually near major rivers in the world. The Middle East and Egypt, and later the Indus Valley, China, Mesoamerica and the Central Andes housed the great Civilization centers. These regions were witnesses of the blossoming of the first city-states and **empires**. On present understanding, it was in **Mesopotamia**, before anywhere else, where major urban centers first developed and where (if not in Egypt) the appearance of writing took place before 3000 BC, a momentous event that inaugurated History.

Thanks to the written word, which was born as a bureaucratic and administrative tool, the human being had the opportunity, for the first time, to record events, calculations and information with certain accuracy. Parallel to this revolutionary invention and the consequential improvement in the **transmission of knowledge**, the specialization of trades took place.

Humanity inherited an extraordinary cultural heritage from this emerging and fascinating first stage of history, which was the basis for, or had powerful influence on, the brilliant succeeding Civilizations of **classical antiquity**, of which in turn later peoples would learn, forging history in all its dazzling diversity over the centuries. Thus, Civilization ended up reaching every corner of the globe, so far from these mighty rivers that cocooned the emergence of precursor Civilizations.

Chronology

	4000 BC	3500 BC	3000 BC	2500 BC	2000
Mesopotamia	Sumer			Akkad	Babylonia Empire
Ancient Egypt				Old Kingdom	Middle Kingdom
India				Indus Civilization	
Hebrew People					
China					Xia Dynasty
Ancient Greece					
Persian Empire					
Celts					
Rome					
Vikings					
Byzantium					
Islam					
Maya					
Aztecs					
Incas					
Japan					

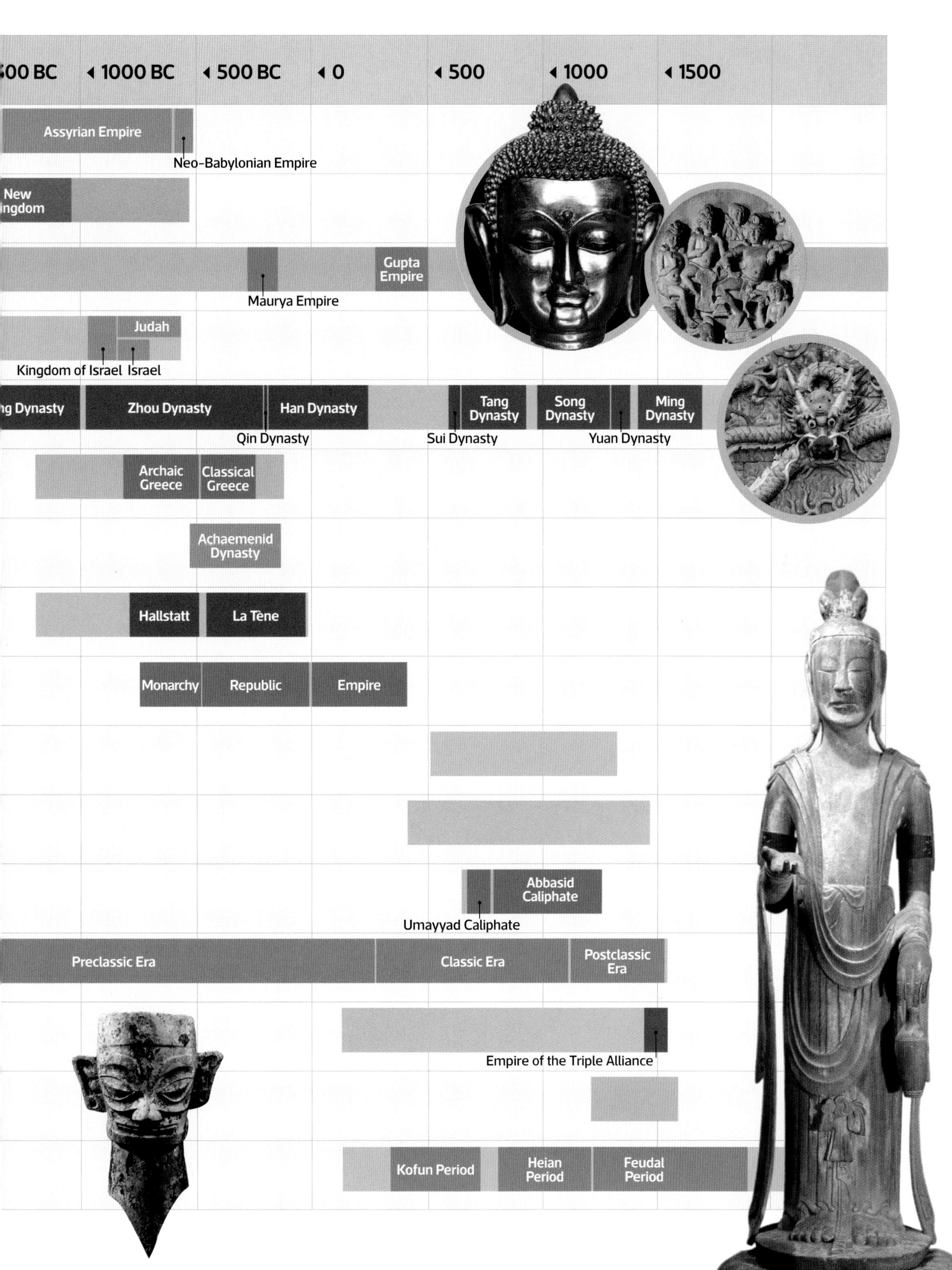

00 BC
1000 BC
500 BC
0
500
1000
1500
Assyrian Empire
Neo-Babylonian Empire
New
ngdom
Gupta
Empire
Maurya Empire
Judah
Kingdom of Israel
Israel
ng Dynasty
Zhou Dynasty
Han Dynasty
Tang
Dynasty
Song
Dynasty
Ming
Dynasty
Qin Dynasty
Sui Dynasty
Yuan Dynasty
Archaic
Greece
Classical
Greece
Achaemenid
Dynasty
Hallstatt
La Tène
Monarchy
Republic
Empire
Abbasid
Caliphate
Umayyad Caliphate
Preclassic Era
Classic Era
Postclassic
Era
Empire of the Triple Alliance
Kofun Period
Heian
Period
Feudal
Period

Chapter 1

Early Civilizations

In southern Mesopotamia, in the alluvial plains of the Tigris and Euphrates, the farmers in the region were gradually congregating in urban centers. These primitive cities, founded by the Sumerian people, soon experienced great prosperity, probably due to the need to channel the swampy lands of the Tigris-Euphrates delta. This was the trigger for public works and, consequently, an exceptional development.

While the Sumerian culture created a city-state model for the first time in history, at the other end of the area known as Fertile Crescent, on the banks of the Nile, another great Civilization of the period of the High Cultures was forged: Egypt. The Egyptians built the first great empire of antiquity, the existence of which lasted for three thousand years and reached its zenith with the New Kingdom (c. 1550-1070 BC).

Also in the Indus River Valley (now Pakistan and north-east India), another river basin hosted a major Civilization, where cities with smart urban planning, such as Mohenjo-Daro or Harappa, peaked towards 2300 BC. In the next millennium, the Hebrew people settled in Canaan, where centuries later the kingdom of Israel arose, leaving an indelible mark in history that has survived to this day.

Mesopotamia

The region between the Tigris and Euphrates rivers was the cradle of not only great inventions such as the wheel, metal work and writing, but also of great myths, as the primeval chaos, the Creation and the Flood.

Towards Sedentary Lifestyles

Between 6000 and 5000 BC there was a momentous revolution in Mesopotamia: thanks to the fertility of the land, both agriculture and livestock breeding were strengthened. It changed from nomadic to sedentary life, and several towns settled in the region.

AKKADIANS
By 2300 B.C. Sargon, king of Akkad, conquered all of Mesopotamia, thus establishing the first empire in history, which lasted a century.

ASSYRIANS
The Assyrian empire started its consolidation around 1300 BC. It reached its apogee in 600 BC, when its power went from Egypt to Elam.

City-States

We tend to speak of a "Mesopotamian Civilization," when, in fact, many peoples coexisted in the region which evolved from hunting and gathering to the establishment of complex societies, trade, new forms of government and a powerful priestly class. Thus, the Mesopotamian city-states were born.

Sphinx. The Assyrians were the creators of the sphinxes bearded like the picture.

BABYLON
The capital of the Babylonian Empire, erected by King Hammurabi in 1800 BC, maintained its splendor for nearly 15 centuries. In the picture we see Ishtar, Babylonian goddess of the sky.

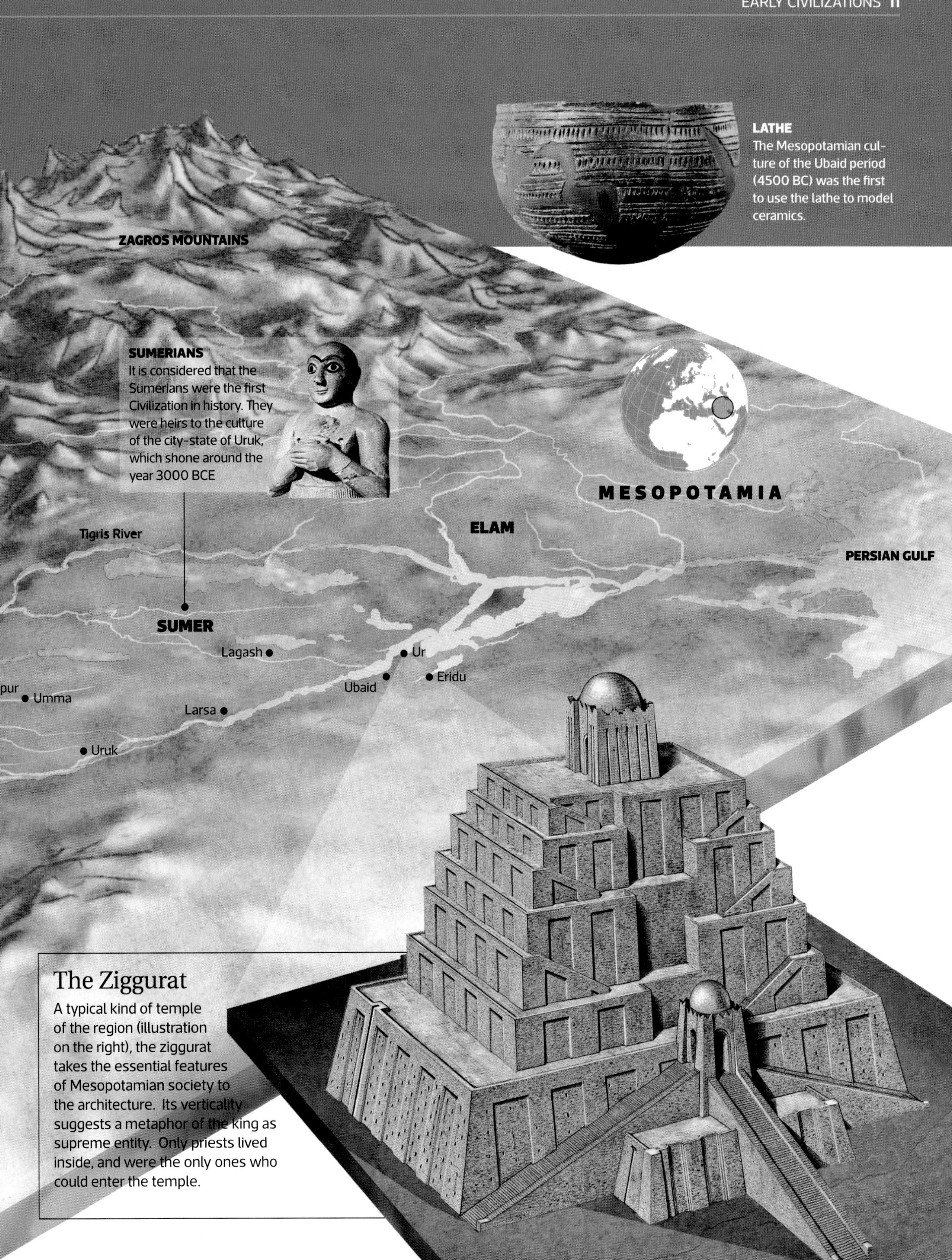

LATHE
The Mesopotamian culture of the Ubaid period (4500 BC) was the first to use the lathe to model ceramics.

SUMERIANS
It is considered that the Sumerians were the first Civilization in history. They were heirs to the culture of the city-state of Uruk, which shone around the year 3000 BCE

The Ziggurat

A typical kind of temple of the region (illustration on the right), the ziggurat takes the essential features of Mesopotamian society to the architecture. Its verticality suggests a metaphor of the king as supreme entity. Only priests lived inside, and were the only ones who could enter the temple.

The Invention of Writing

What began as a tool to count stored products and to regulate commercial transactions in Mesopotamia, eventually resulted in the most significant invention for Humanity, writing, a starting point in history.

History Begins

Writing is the system of graphic representation of a language by means of engraved or drawn signs. First, there was the ideographic script (expression of ideas) and then, phonetics (representing sounds). The Sumerians were the first to develop it, towards 3300 BC.

PRACTICES
Tablets have been found containing the practices of "callig-raphy" performed in some temples made by those aspiring to become scribes.

THE "HYMN OF NIDABA"
The Sumerian scribes transcribed the hymns that the priests recited in religious celebrations, such as the "Hymn of Nidaba," which narrates the destruction of the city of Ur at the hands of the god Enlil.

Clay and Wood

Cuneiform writing is one of the oldest forms of ideographic writing. For its tracing, a punch and a clay tablet, such as those in the drawing, were used. It was named after the wedge-shaped mark left by the stylus when pressed on the tablet.

EVOLUTION OF WRITING CUNEIFORM

Sign	3200 BC	3000 BC	2500 BC	2300 BC	Assyria
God					
Woman					
Fish					
Water					
Ox					

Sumerian Weight. It is shaped zoomorphic.

Weights and Measures

The need to organize production and trade led, in addition to writing, to a system of weights and measures which allowed counting gold and silver, metals with exchange value in Mesopotamia, Asia Minor and Egypt.

Heroic Deeds and Campaigns

This tablet, found in the ruins of Uruk, is one of the oldest in Mesopotamia. It shows signs of a numeric character -circles- and very primitive pictograms. The names of Uruk and Dilmun, a small kingdom of the peripheral Assyrian empire, were found. It narrates an heroic deed by Akkadian king Sargon in the eighth century BC.

EVOLUTION
Based on the phonograms, the signs came to represent the sounds of whole words and syllables.

PICTOGRAMS
The Sumerians used virtually 2,000 pictograms. To write 'woman,' for example, they drew an inverted triangle.

PHONOGRAMS
The scribes started combining different signs for their phonetic value, which facilitated the writing of any word.

The Code of Hammurabi

This famous stele has the inscription of court decisions made by Babylonian King Hammurabi. It dates back to 1792 BC and it is one of the first compilations of laws of antiquity. In Mesopotamia, the laws were attributed a divine origin.

The Legal Unity of the Kingdom

King Hammurabi, sovereign of the first Babylonian Empire, believed that the body of laws of the territory had to be put in writing to please the gods, although, unlike other monarchs, he did not consider himself to be related to them. Hammurabi ordered the placement of several replicas of his code throughout the kingdom, aware that legal homogenization of the territory would ensure its unity.

HAMMURABI'S WORLD
World Map of the period of Hammurabi, self-proclaimed "King of the Four Quarters," referring to the four cardinal points. The circle was a symbolic representation of power.

WOMEN
The Code of Hammurabi laws barely refer to women. But they do mention the cases of adultery and incest, which are considered a crime.

Woman weaving. Relief in terracotta from the second millennium BC.

CAPITAL PUNISHMENT
This relief found in the ruins of the city-state of Tutub shows the execution of a death sentence in Mesopotamia.

The Law of Retaliation

The so-called law of retaliation, which in the book of Leviticus (XXIV, 17-23) of the Old Testament is summed up with the phrase "an eye for an eye and a tooth for a tooth," was already present in the Code of Hammurabi. Certain parts of the Mosaic Law are similar to laws of the Code, so some scholars have argued that the Hebrews derived their law from the Babylonian one. However, other experts do not share this view.

THE DISCOVERY
An archaeological expedition found the stele in Elam (current Iran) in 1901. It was taken to Paris, where it was translated. It is currently kept in the Louvre Museum.

DIVINE ORIGIN
The top shows the time the Babylonian king receives the code from Shamash, the chief god of the city of Lagash.

INSCRIPTIONS
Most of the monolith is occupied by laws inscribed in cuneiform Akkadian characters.

Content

Its laws govern issues such as theft, damage to property, marriage, rights of minors, the relationship with slaves and murder. Punishment varies according to the type of offender and victim.

THE MONOLITH
The Code of Hammurabi is a basalt stele of 2.25 m high.

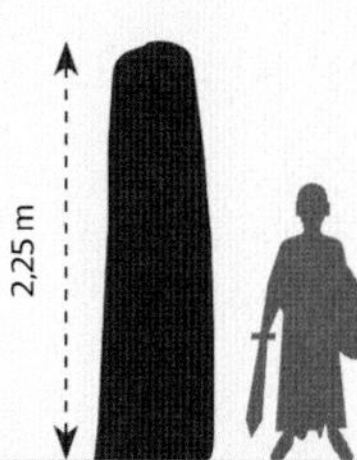

Standards

The Code of Hammurabi contains case law provisions of criminal and civil nature. Numbered from 1 to 282 (except for numbers 13, 66-99 and 110-111, which are missing), the laws set different rules for everyday life. Find some examples below:

1 CRIMINAL LAW

- **Law 1.** "If a man bring an accusation against a man, and charge him with a (capital) crime, but cannot prove it, he, the accuser, shall be put to death."
- **Law 25.** "If a fire break out in a man's house and a man who goes to extinguish it casts his eye on the furniture of the owner of the house, and take the furniture of the owner of the house, that man shall be thrown into that fire."
- **Law 196.** "If a man destroy the eye of another man, they shall destroy his eye."
- **Law 229.** "If a builder build a house for a man and do not make its construction firm, and the house which he has built collapse and cause the death of the owner of the house, that builder shall be put to death."

2 CIVIL LAW

- **Law 53.** "If a man neglect to strengthen his dyke and do not strengthen it, and a break be made in his dyke and the water carry away the farm-land, the man in whose dyke the break has been made shall restore the grain which he has damaged."
- **Law 131.** "If a man accuse his wife and she has not been taken in lying with another man, she shall take an oath in the name of god and she shall return to her house."
- **Law 134.**"If a man be captured and there no be maintenance in his house and his wife enter into another house, that woman has no blame."

The Splendor of Babylon

Herodotus of Halicarnassus, a great traveller who is regarded as the first historian, wrote: "Of all the cities of Mesopotamia, the most famous and strongest one was Babylon, with a magnificence that eclipsed that of any city we have ever known."

The Second Empire

During the reigns of Nabopolassar (626 BC-605 BC), founder of the Neo-Babylonian Empire, and his son Nebuchadnezzar (605 BC-562 BC), Babylon became the main city of Mesopotamia. Both monarchs undertook great public works and erected fortifications and palaces. From this period, the Ishtar Gate is highlighted. It is the most important of the eight monumental gates of the inner wall of the city.

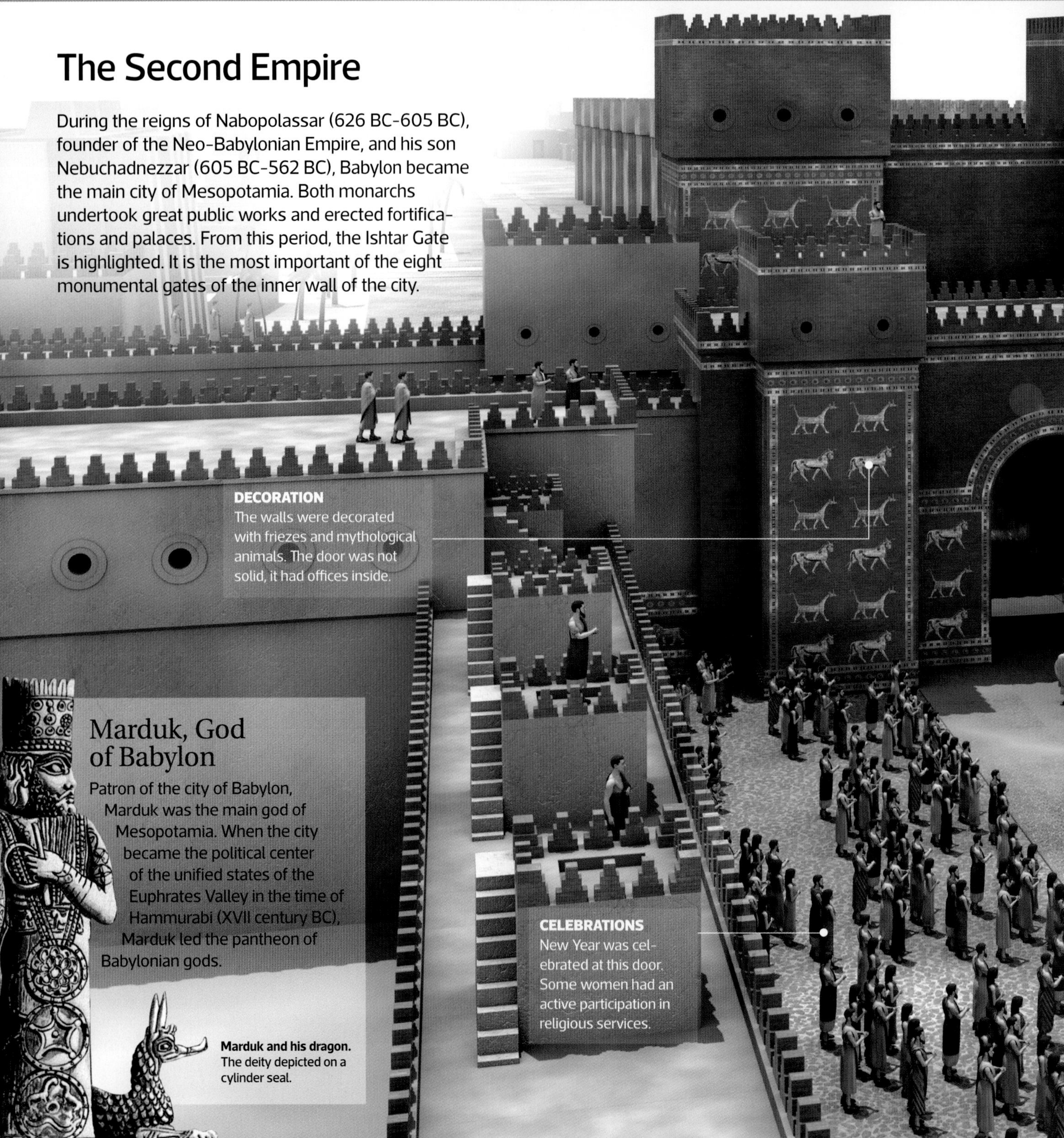

DECORATION
The walls were decorated with friezes and mythological animals. The door was not solid, it had offices inside.

CELEBRATIONS
New Year was celebrated at this door. Some women had an active participation in religious services.

Marduk, God of Babylon

Patron of the city of Babylon, Marduk was the main god of Mesopotamia. When the city became the political center of the unified states of the Euphrates Valley in the time of Hammurabi (XVII century BC), Marduk led the pantheon of Babylonian gods.

Marduk and his dragon. The deity depicted on a cylinder seal.

WINGED LION
The symbol of Babylon was the winged lion, representing the power of the city and its armies. It was extensively present in the Ishtar Gate, in glazed brick mosaics such as in the picture.

The Ishtar Gate. Recreation of this entry in the walls of Babylon.

ROUTE OF THE PROCESSIONS
Ishtar Gate was the origin of this important street that ran through the city, past the palace of Nebuchadnezzar, and arrived at the New Year temple.

IN RUINS
The door remains were found by a team of German archaeologists. After being rebuilt, they are currently exhibited in Berlin.

Ancient Egypt

The Egyptian Civilization could not have built a nation like the one it developed from 3200 BC without the Nile. Its swelling and the fertility of its banks fueled a political and economic structure and even a conception of life and death.

The Sacred Clay

Every year in mid-July, the Nile began to rise. The flood covered the sandy soils and, when it retreated, it left a layer of dark mud. The Egyptians called it "black earth" and it was that same earth which prompted the development of agriculture and the sedentary lifestyle of local tribes. The fertile lands met all the needs posed by everyday life, from the grains being transformed into bread, up to the lotus flowers becoming perfume. The same silt nourished rattan reeds, from which the papyrus was made to leave the mark of an unparalleled Civilization in history.

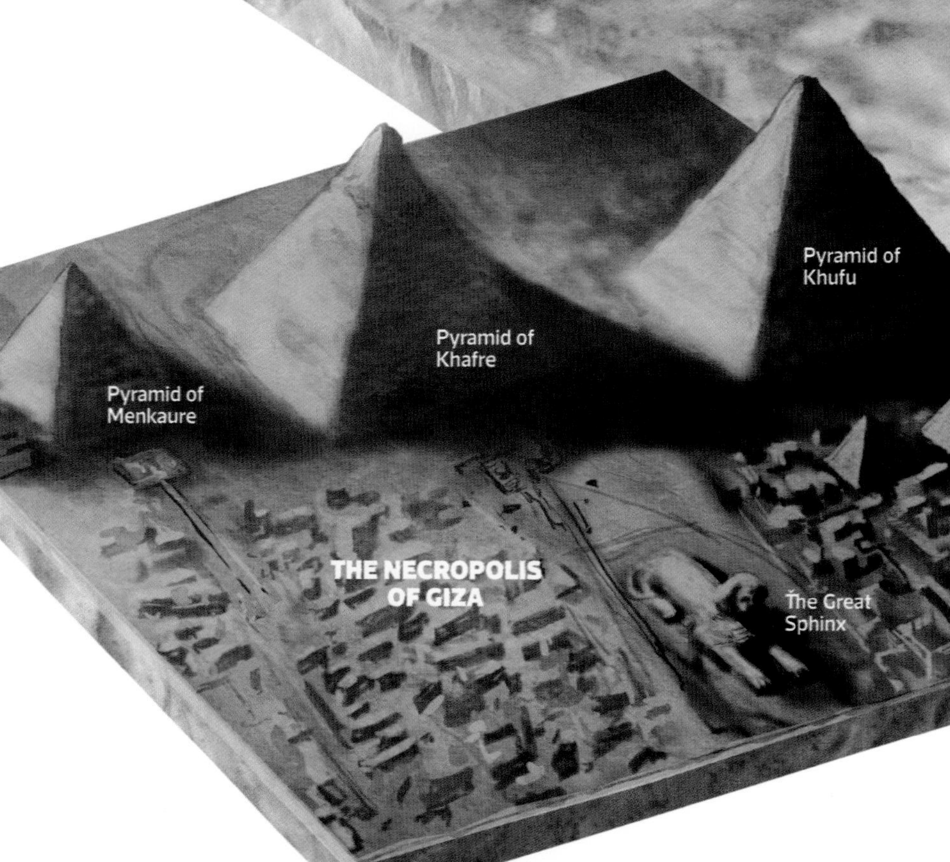

The Giza Plateau

Over 4,000 years ago, at the Giza plateau, the three great pyramids of the Pharaohs Khufu, Khafre and Menkaure of the Fourth Dynasty were erected. They are part of the great necropolis of Memphis, which extended over more than 40 km, and guard the remains of Egyptian kings.

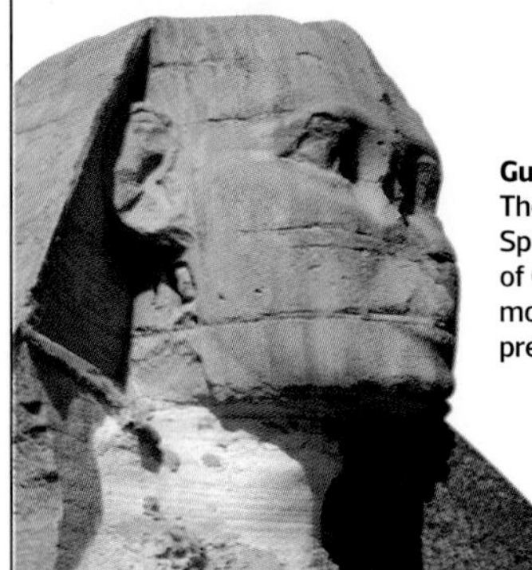

Guardian. The Great Sphinx of Giza monitors the precinct.

Northern Prosperity

The delta of the Nile, the lands of which were the most fertile of the entire river, concentrated the greatest wealth in Lower Egypt. The north had another great advantage: the exit of the Empire to the Mediterranean, scene of large commercial traffic and preferred destination of the ships that were circulating on the Nile.

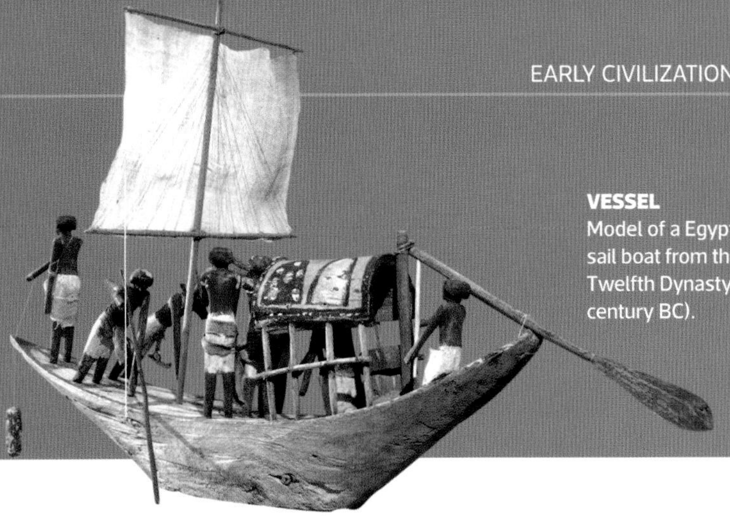

VESSEL
Model of a Egyptian sail boat from the Twelfth Dynasty (22th century BC).

An Indelible Mark

The beer, papyrus, ink, different methods of navigation and the sundial are some of the many contributions of the Civilization of Ancient Egypt to the humankind.

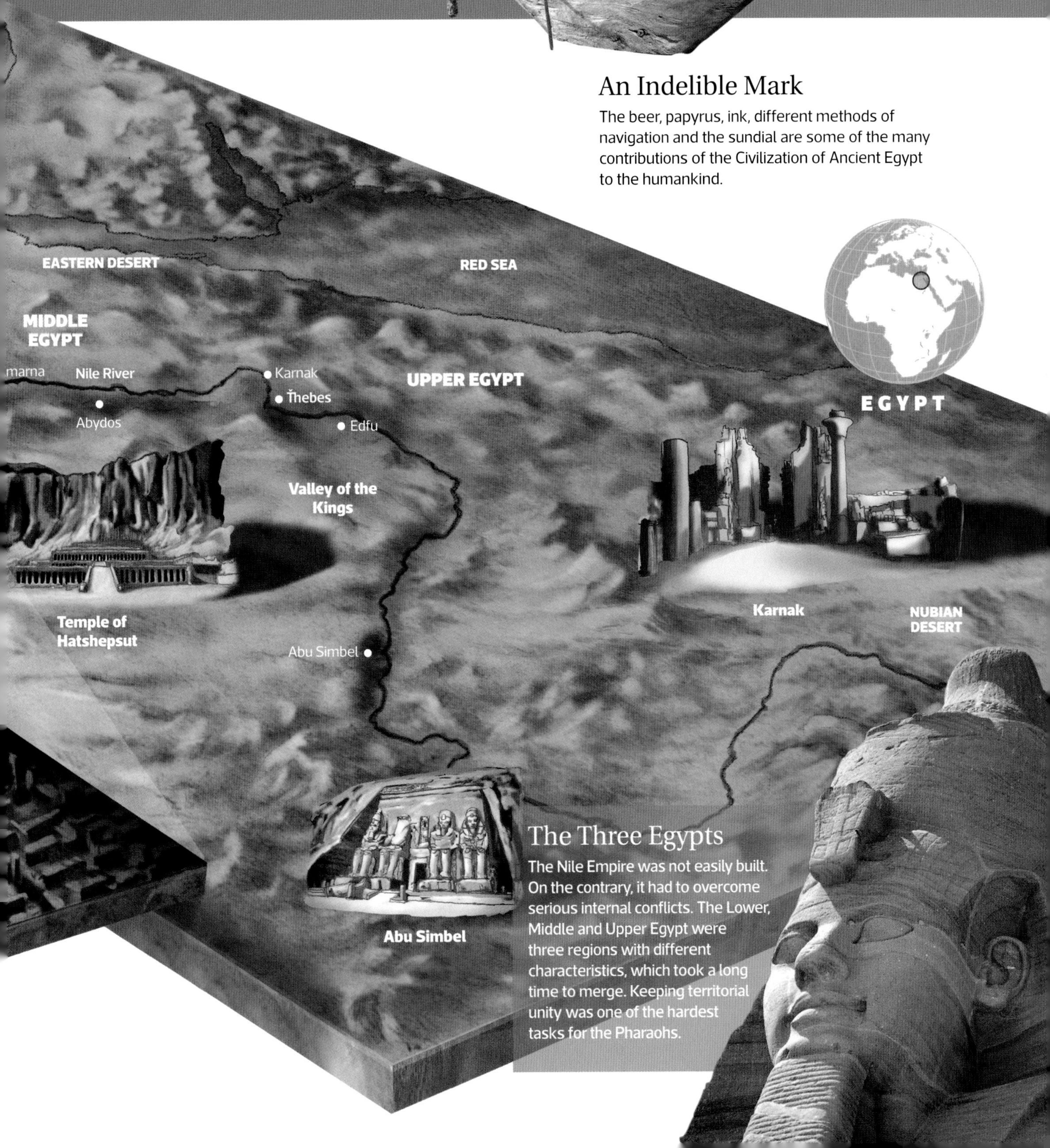

EASTERN DESERT
RED SEA
MIDDLE EGYPT
marna
Nile River
Abydos
Karnak
Thebes
UPPER EGYPT
Edfu
EGYPT
Valley of the Kings
Temple of Hatshepsut
Karnak
NUBIAN DESERT
Abu Simbel
Abu Simbel

The Three Egypts

The Nile Empire was not easily built. On the contrary, it had to overcome serious internal conflicts. The Lower, Middle and Upper Egypt were three regions with different characteristics, which took a long time to merge. Keeping territorial unity was one of the hardest tasks for the Pharaohs.

Egyptian Society

As the incarnation of the god Horus, the Pharaoh in Ancient Egypt exercised absolute power. The nobility and the priests completed the top of the social pyramid. Below were the scribes, soldiers, merchants, laborers and slaves.

The Ruling Caste

The Pharaoh was the owner of the fate of his subjects and of his own human and divine condition, the interlocutor of the gods and the intermediary between them and the earthly beings. But the Empire's internal tensions, especially between Lower and Upper Egypt, and the conflicts with other kingdoms forced the sovereign to adopt a policy of alliances which, in fact, implied a transfer of power. The ancient manors, the clergy and the military caste conspire constantly against the system, which was sharply centralist.

PRIESTS
Located on an almost immediately lower step to that occupied by the Pharaoh and his family, they had the administration of the temples and their lands in their hands. They were devoted to the celebration of worship.

Meryre. The high priest, Meryre, and his wife, Tener.

SLAVES
Probably in Ancient Egypt, slavery did not exist as understood in Greece or Rome, as it is known that slaves had rights and a salary.

Ramesses II. The Pharaoh during the Battle of Kadesh (2003 BC).

Military Power

Egypt needed to have armies, capable of waging battle on several fronts simultaneously. The military was also able to guarantee the unity of the Empire. Uprisings were common by local forces, eager to achieve greater autonomy, so that Pharaoh had to appeal to his political ability and military force to maintain power.

1 Chariots
Pulled by a horse, they were the combat mobile units. They were ridden by a driver and an archer.

2 Archery
It was also a religious activity: at some parties, the Pharaoh threw arrows at the four cardinal points.

3 Pharaoh
Chief of the army, which had generals and intermediate officers. The officers carried a baton.

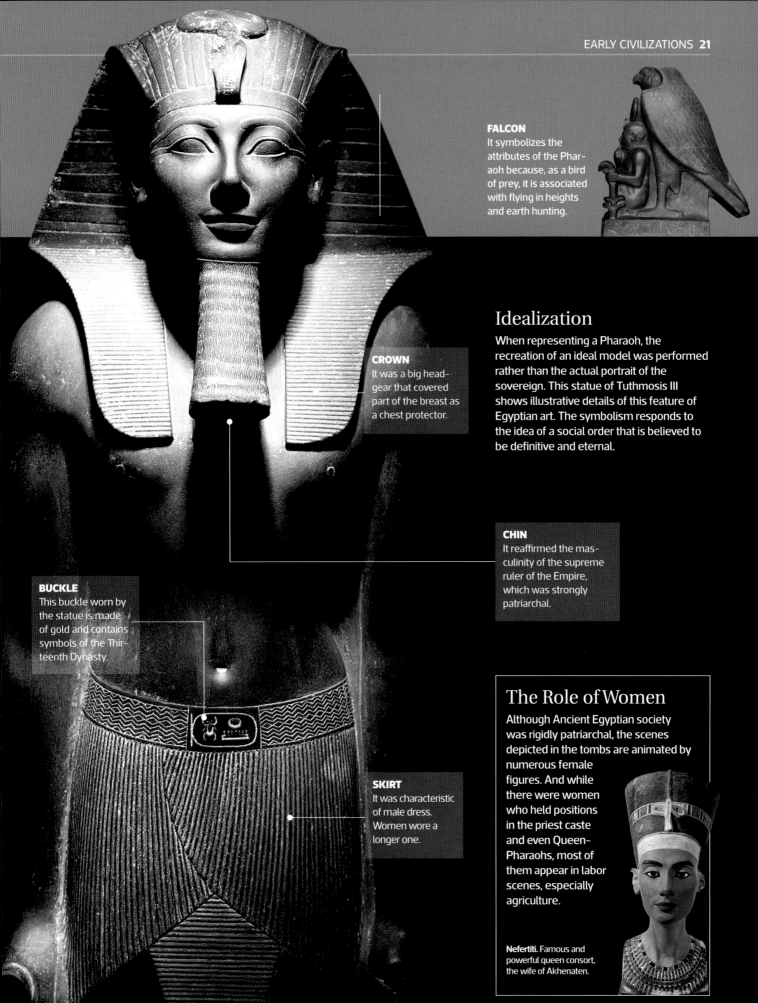

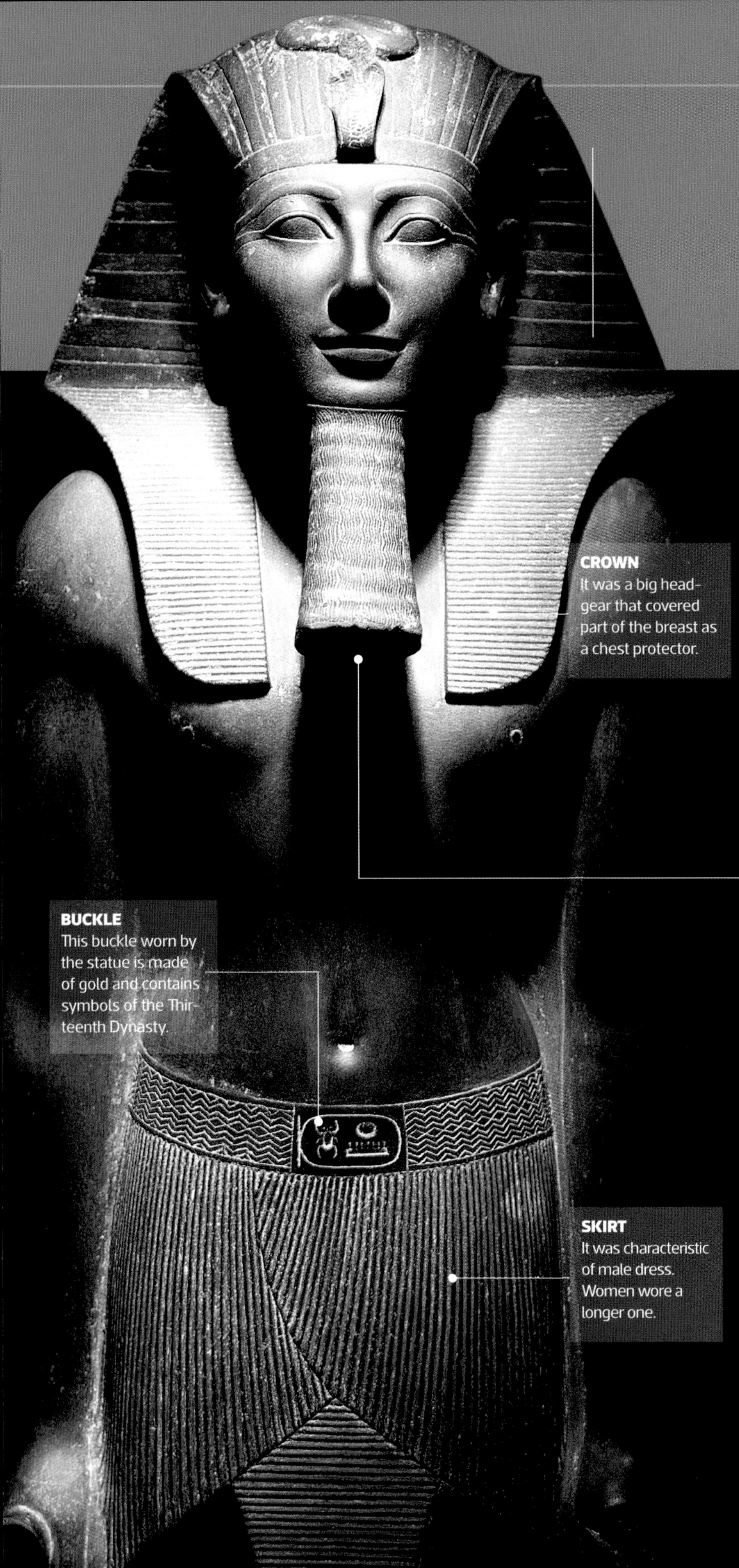

FALCON
It symbolizes the attributes of the Pharaoh because, as a bird of prey, it is associated with flying in heights and earth hunting.

Idealization

When representing a Pharaoh, the recreation of an ideal model was performed rather than the actual portrait of the sovereign. This statue of Tuthmosis III shows illustrative details of this feature of Egyptian art. The symbolism responds to the idea of a social order that is believed to be definitive and eternal.

CROWN
It was a big headgear that covered part of the breast as a chest protector.

CHIN
It reaffirmed the masculinity of the supreme ruler of the Empire, which was strongly patriarchal.

BUCKLE
This buckle worn by the statue is made of gold and contains symbols of the Thirteenth Dynasty.

SKIRT
It was characteristic of male dress. Women wore a longer one.

The Role of Women

Although Ancient Egyptian society was rigidly patriarchal, the scenes depicted in the tombs are animated by numerous female figures. And while there were women who held positions in the priest caste and even Queen-Pharaohs, most of them appear in labor scenes, especially agriculture.

Nefertiti. Famous and powerful queen consort, the wife of Akhenaten.

The Hieroglyphs

In the Ancient Egypt, the god Thoth was attributed handling the knowledge of the written word to humans. For over 3,000 years, the Egyptians used a system with more than 6,000 hieroglyphic signs, which could not be deciphered until 1822.

A Complex System

By the year 3000 BC, Egyptian writing began to use a pictographic system similar to that of Mesopotamia and, in fact, it is likely that traders in that region introduced the use of writing in Egypt. Eventually it derived into a hieroglyphic phonetic system, which became widespread for administrative and religious uses. It combined ideographic and consonant elements. Its usage was reserved for a caste of officers, i.e. the scribes and, therefore, only a select few were literate.

STYLE
Most of the representations of animals are naturalistic drawings, but there also is an abundance of fantastic animals.

KNOTS
In hieroglyphic writing, certain knots in rope reeds represented the name of the Pharaoh.

DETERMINATIVE SIGNS
They integrated hieroglyphic writing as special signs, intended to clarify the meaning when it was ambiguous.

The Hieratic Script

It arose as a simplification of the hieroglyphic system, which was more complicated and time consuming. Gradually, the hieratic characters wandered off from the drawings and their writing started to be linked together, adding the use of red dots as a sign to separate phrases. Its simple nature facilitated the spread of writing and the number of scribes increased.

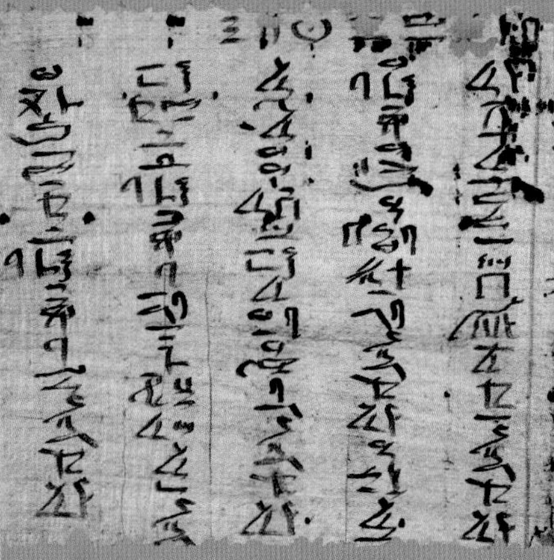

Papyrus. Fragment covered with hieratic script.

Guardians of the Word

The scribes were a privileged elite in charge of writing the sacred texts, letters, reports and surveys. They did it on papyrus, with special sticks. They studied in specialized schools that depended on the temples, given that their job was considered religious in nature. It was common for them to inherit the position and to be part of the same lineage.

SCRIBE
Sculpture of a scribe of the Fourth or Fifth Egyptian Dynasty (2600-2350 BC).

ANIMAL FIGURES
They were very frequent as hieroglyphic signs and each corresponded to a different phoneme. For example, the owl was equivalent to the sound "em."

OTHER MEDIA
Tablets with hieroglyphs that belonged to the Pharaoh Amenhotep. They date back to around 1379-1362 BC.

IDEOGRAMS
Also called "pictograms," they combined with other signs to express concepts, ideas, etc.

PHONOGRAMS
Signs that served as transposition of simple sounds equivalent to the modern alphabet.

Thousands of Variations

Thanks to archaeology, we now know, for instance, that the number of hieroglyphs reached over 6,000. To make their study easier, from the twentieth century, the list known as Gardiner's Sign List is applied, through which the British Egyptologist Alan Gardiner (1879-1963) cataloged 743 basic hieroglyphics, ranked in 26 subgroups, such as crafts, mythology, body parts, etc.

Thot. Represented with the head of ibis, a wading bird, it was the guardian deity of writing.

The Indian Civilization

Despite its vastness, the Indian subcontinent is a region bounded by the great mountainous wall in the north and the sea that surrounds it. This unity facilitated the development of a Civilization common to the various ethnic groups that endorsed this scenario.

Rivers of Life

The high fertility of the lands in India favored that the nomadic tribes adopted a sedentary lifestyle and laid the foundation of a new Civilization. On the banks and the mouths of great rivers (the Indus, the Ganges and their tributaries) major urban centers emerged, which became centers of wealth, refinement and power. And those same rivers served as communication routes for trade and exchange.

MADRAS

Indus River

THAR DESERT

Ceremonial Temple

The colossal temples known as stupas were proof of the greatness of Indian Civilization. The Stupa of Sanchi, one of the oldest, was built around the third century BC and erected to protect Buddha relics. Its hemispherical structure is surrounded by a processional road and a stone balustrade in which there are four access doors.

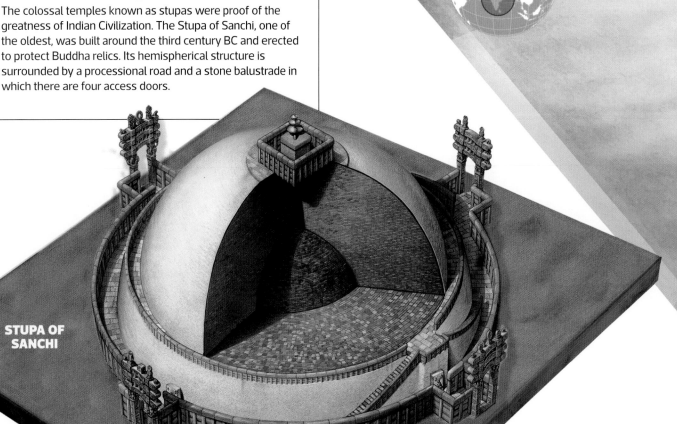

Religion and Philosophy

The ancient Indian Civilization was especially fruitful in religious and philosophical matters. Even today, their culture works as a strong counterweight to the Western world-view.

Shore Temple. One of sacred buildings in the Mamallapuram city.

BUDDHIST MONK
Detail of the paintings of the Ajanta Caves, dating from the centuries II BC to VIII AD.

The First Empire

The kings of the Maurya Dynasty (c. 320-180 BC) were the first to centrally exercise power in India, providing it with a state administration that gen erated an Indian national feeling. The engine of that historic achievement was the founder of the dynasty, Chandragupta. Later, his grandson Asoka underpinned that heritage and Buddhism became the religion of the Mauryan Empire.

Kussara art. After the fall of the Mauryan Empire, the Kussara Dynasty established a thriving kingdom in the north.

The Indus Culture

The cities of the Indus River basin were the first Civilization in India and Pakistan. In these fertile lands, a unique culture flourished that stood out for its excellent urban planning and an active trade that reached Mesopotamia.

A Vast Influence

The Indus Civilization, the first one that emerged in South Asia, crowned the development of Neolithic cultures that flourished from mid-seventh millennium BC in North-western India and in Pakistan, in the regions of Balochistan, Sindh and Punjab. It reached its peak with the construction of cities in the valleys of the Indus, the Civilization role of which was similar to that of the Nile in Egypt and the Tigris and Euphrates in Mesopotamia. It exerted an important cultural influence that reached the borders of current Iran and Afghanistan.

REFINEMENT
The female figurines from Harappa are more delicate and suggestive that the ancient goddesses of fertility.

Chronology

The fertility of the lands of the Indus did not require the costly irrigation works of the arid Mesopotamia. In turn, it allowed the accumulation of surpluses and the diversification of products and activities.

6500 BC — Neolithic
Early stages of the Neolithic settlement of Mehrgarh, the first cultural center in Baluchistan.

3500 BC — Evolution
Villages of Quetta, Rhana Rungai and Mundigak. Semi-nomadic pastoral activities.

3000 BC — Amri
Cities of the Amri culture (Pre-Harappa). Settlements of farmers in the Indus valley.

2700 BC — Kalibangan
Apogee of the Kalibangan city on the banks of the sacred Sarasvati River, which has dried up.

2500 BC — Trade
Rise and expansion of the cities of Harappa and Mohenjo-Daro. Trade with Mesopotamia.

1800 BC — Decline
The downfall of Harappa begins. The first urban cultures emerge in the Ganges River valley.

1500 BC — Collapse
Invasion of the Aryans and destruction of Mohenjo-Daro. Cultures of Jhangra and Jhukar.

Chess Cradle?

Persians and Arabs have a dispute over the paternity of chess, but archaeological findings in Harappa suggest that a variety of this game was played thousands of years ago, by several people, in the valleys of the Indus.

SCULPTURE
The terracotta figures found in Harappa and other centers provided information on the life and wildlife of the Indus region.

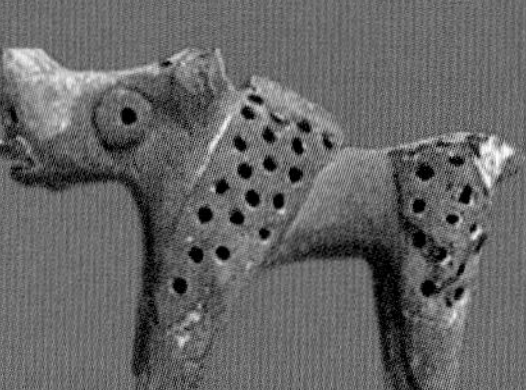

Disappearance

The reasons for the collapse of this Civilization, which could be due to climate change or a change in the course of the river around 1600 BC, are not known with certainty.

Writing

The Indus culture had its own system of writing, from which 20 characters and over 500 signs are known (some of which relate to Tamil, a language still spoken in India), and were used in commercial seals and places of worship.

Examples. Some of the signs used by this culture. Exact meaning is unknown.

DIVERSIFICATION
Agriculture was combined with the grazing of donkeys, oxen and buffaloes and with the textile industry, metal-lurgy and pottery.

AGRICULTURE
Periodic floods and the river silt fertilized the valley lands and led to the prolif-eration of crops and vegetation.

Big Planned Cities

The main cities of the Indus Civilization were Mojenho-Daro (the largest of all), Harappa and Lothal. Built during the Bronze Age in Punjab, Harappa (see picture) reached a population of 25,000 people, with neighborhoods differentiated by the trades.

Dimensions. At its peak, Harappa spread over more than a hundred hectares.

The Legacy of India

The Civilizations of the Indus and Ganges were permeable to outside influences, and laid the foundations for a rich culture that spread across the subcontinent.

Racially-mixed Society

The crossing between the ancient original Vedic religion in the basins of the Indus and the Ganges and the many peoples that later influenced the territory gave birth in India to religions as influential or of long standing such as Buddhism, Hinduism and Jainism. These religions have been closely linked to the philosophical systems and fostered most art forms of India.

Buddhism

This is a religion that is not theistic nor a dogma and comes from the ancient Vedas, in which each individual must see for himself the Master's teachings. Actually, many consider it a philosophy.

BUDDHA, THE "ENLIGHTENED ONE"
Buddhism is based on the teachings of Siddhartha Gautama (fifth century BC), who gave himself to meditation to become the Buddha, meaning "the Enlightened One."

Hinduism

More than just a religion, it is a religious tradition that has existed for 5,000 years comprising different faiths, numerous gods and a sum of metaphysical and religious beliefs, cults, in addition to rituals and customs.

Vishnu. Deity of the Vedic age, Hinduism turned him into the supreme deity.

Jainism

In contrast to Hinduism, this religion does not accept the Vedic (sacred) texts or the authority of the Brahmin priests. Through its practice, and doctrine, sacrifices are made to ensure that the soul reaches a divine consciousness, overcoming inner demons.

INFLUENCE
Hinduism spread throughout Southwest Asia. This sculpture of the Four Heads of Brahma is in the temple of Angkor (Cambodia).

The Trimurti

In the context of Hinduism, the god Brahma, which in Sanskrit means "development" or "evolution," is the creator god and a member of the Trimurti, the triad comprising Brahma, as creator god, Vishnu, the protector god, and Shiva, the destroyer god.

Philosophy

Indian philosophical systems aim not only to interpret the world, but they also outline theories targeted at the salvation of individual and social life. They all focus on the relationships between three main concepts: the *atman* or individual self; the *karma* or set of activities performed by the human being; and the *moksha*, the liberation state. They also agree on the unity of body and spirit.

Prayer wheel

Bhagavata Purana. Illustrated old edition.

Sanskrit literature

During the classical period (200 BC - 1100 AD), with the already codified Sanskrit language, a kind of literature was born that adapted Vedic legends to new genres of non-sacred nature. The Puranas, poetic tales of epic style, stand out among others, with some first authors such as Kalidasa, Bhartrhari and Bhavabhuti.

Art and religion

The stupa is one of the embematic references of Indian art . It began as a burial mound with a semicircular construction surrounded by a stone fence. As from the Maurya dynasty, it became a religious temple. The most famous stupa is that of Sanchi.

ARCHITECTURAL EVOLUTION

Stupa

- **Origin:** India sixth century BC.
- Simple hemispherical dome on one or two circular basement floors.

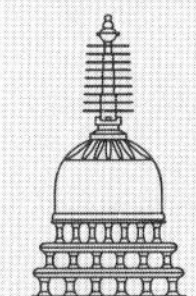

Chorten

- **Origin:** Tibet fifth century AD.
- Stupa in which the dome and the pillar acquire conical shape. It has more levels.

The Hebrew People

In the region that the Bible denominates Canaan and the Romans called Palestine in Middle East, the Hebrew culture flourished 3,500 years ago. The sacred book of Christianity tells its story, which begins with the arrival of the patriarch Abraham to Canaan.

Journey to Canaan

Nomadic pastoralists of Mesopotamian origin, the Hebrews settled in Canaan before 1500 BC led by Abraham and organized in patriarchal families. They were dedicated to livestock, agriculture and trade. With time, a system of city-states was put in place and, in 1025 BC, the Kingdom of Israel was established. As a land of transit, it was always subject to invasions, exiles and returns.

CYPRUS

MEDITERRANEAN SEA

ISRAEL
The part of the kingdom that kept the name Israel (or Northern Kingdom following the rejection of the Ten Tribes from the North to King Rehoboam and his division) existed between 930 BC and 720 BC, when it was conquered by the Assyrian people.

The Holy Sepulchre

In the city of Jerusalem stands the Basilica of the Holy Sepulchre, inside which there supposedly are the sites of the Crucifixion and Resurrection of Jesus Christ. Its recovery from the hands of Islam was the pretext put forward by the papacy and by the Christian kingdoms to justify the Crusades, medieval military campaigns that led to mass killings and destruction.

The basilica. It was completed in 335 AD, under the reign of Emperor Constantine.

THE HOLY SEPULCHRE

The Temple of Solomon

King Solomon ordered the erection of a temple in Jerusalem (recreation in the picture), where he kept the Ark of the Covenant which contained the Tablets of Law that God gave to Moses. Destroyed twice (by the Babylonians and the Romans), today there is only its western wall standing: the Wailing Wall.

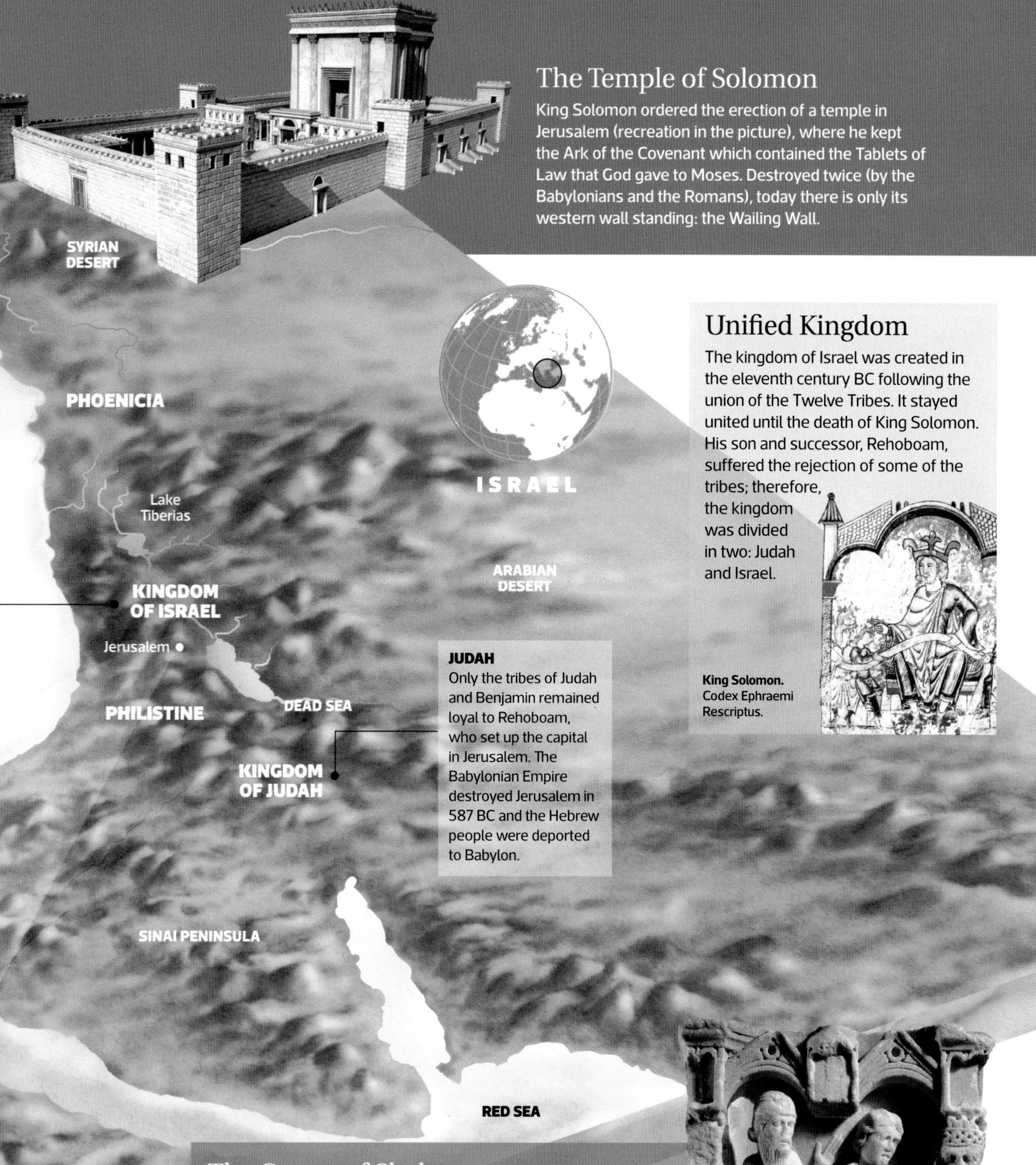

Unified Kingdom

The kingdom of Israel was created in the eleventh century BC following the union of the Twelve Tribes. It stayed united until the death of King Solomon. His son and successor, Rehoboam, suffered the rejection of some of the tribes; therefore, the kingdom was divided in two: Judah and Israel.

King Solomon. Codex Ephraemi Rescriptus.

JUDAH
Only the tribes of Judah and Benjamin remained loyal to Rehoboam, who set up the capital in Jerusalem. The Babylonian Empire destroyed Jerusalem in 587 BC and the Hebrew people were deported to Babylon.

The Queen of Sheba

According to the Old Testament, the queen of the land of Sheba (current Ethiopia) went to Jerusalem with a large entourage in order to learn about the wisdom attributed to Israeli King Solomon (right, in a capital). She brought gifts of spices, gold and precious stones. According to the biblical version, the queen was so impressed by the justice imparted by Solomon that she converted to monotheism.

The Kings of Israel

The period from Abraham's covenant with God until the formation of a kingdom for his people was fraught with obstacles, slavery and diasporas that marked the Hebrews, for whom exercising their memory is a mandate.

The Promised Land

According to the biblical story, Abraham was the founder of the first monotheistic religion and, the same time, father (patriarch) of the Hebrew people. Son of a sculptor of idols, Abraham lived in the Mesopotamian city of Ur where (between 1900-1500 BC) he was called by God and sealed a pact with him: in exchange for abandoning his land and his family, Abraham would be the patriarch of a large offspring, which would receive the land of Canaan in perpetuity in exchange for respecting Yahweh as the one God of his people.

THE DESCENDANTS
Abraham and his wife Sarah gave birth to Isaac, who in turn was the father of Jacob. God was faithful to his promise and Isaac had a brood of 12 children, which gave rise to the Twelve Tribes of Israel.

From the Patriarchs to the Kingdom of Israel

The direction of the Hebrew people initially fell into the hands of the patriarchs. After Moses led the Twelve Tribes to Canaan, a few leaders called judges were chosen, until the kingdom of Israel was finally created. The kings of the unified kingdom of Israel were Saul, Ish-bosheth, David and Solomon.

Moses, the Spiritual Father
Through him, God delivered to the Hebrew people the Tablets of Law, with the Ten Commandments that it must follow. According to the Bible, under the guidance of prophet Moses, the people of Israel were freed from slavery around 1250 BC and marched from Egypt to the Promised Land. Moses, whose existence is not confirmed, died before getting there.

David, the Poet King
After reaching the Promised Land, Twelve Judges were responsible for the administration of the territory until the nation was consolidated and the kingdom of Israel was born. Saul was the first king, followed by King David who turned Jerusalem into the capital city and made Israel shine. The Psalms, the Bible's religious poetry, are part oh his work.

King Solomon
Son of David, Solomon was anointed king of Israel in 970 BC. In his youth he wrote the famous love poem "Song of Songs" of the Bible. It was he who ordered the construction of the famous Temple of Jerusalem. In 931 BC Rehoboam his son succeeded him, but ten of the Twelve Tribes did not recognize his authority, so the kingdom was divided into two: Judah and Israel.

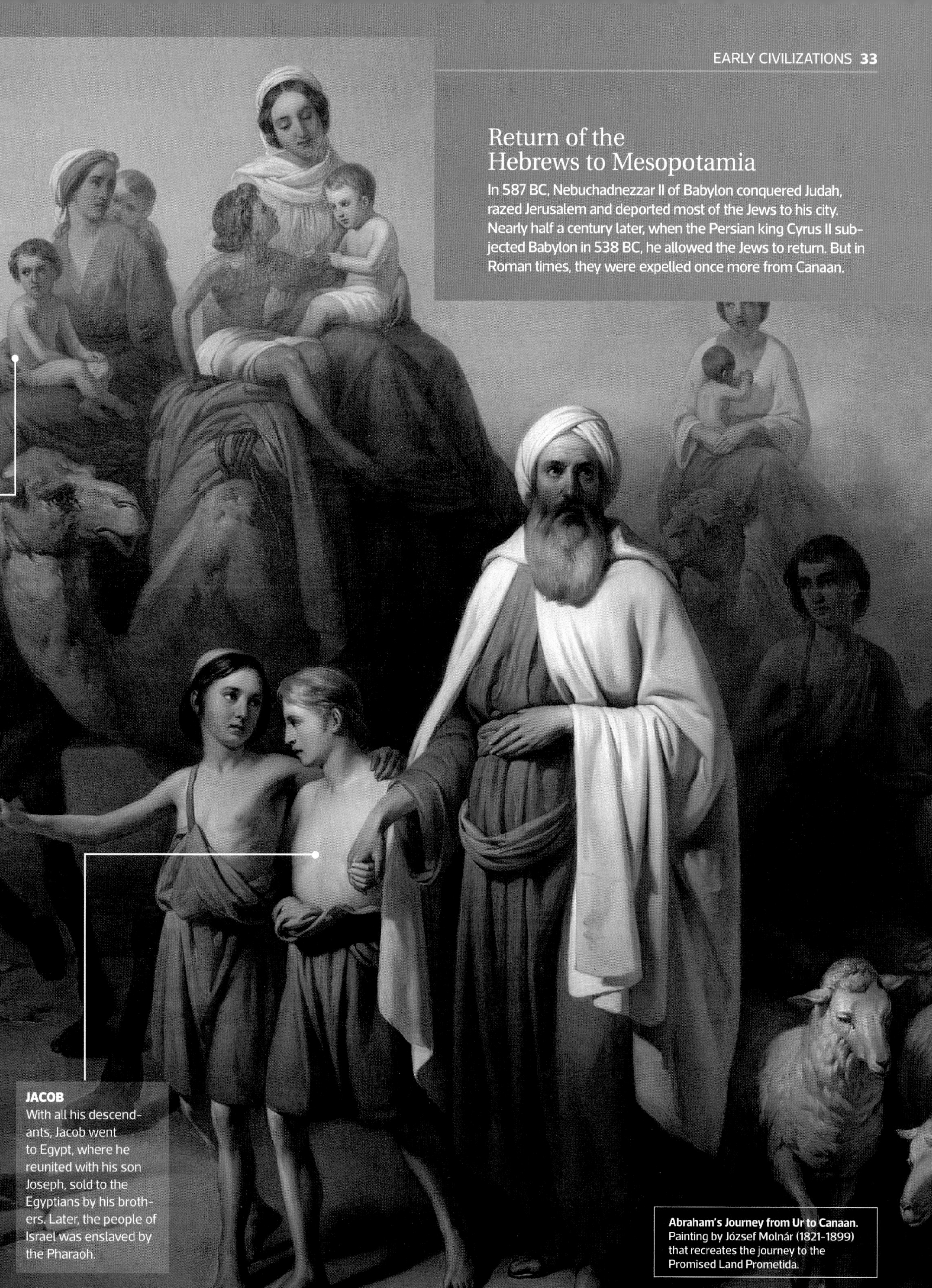

Return of the Hebrews to Mesopotamia

In 587 BC, Nebuchadnezzar II of Babylon conquered Judah, razed Jerusalem and deported most of the Jews to his city. Nearly half a century later, when the Persian king Cyrus II subjected Babylon in 538 BC, he allowed the Jews to return. But in Roman times, they were expelled once more from Canaan.

JACOB
With all his descendants, Jacob went to Egypt, where he reunited with his son Joseph, sold to the Egyptians by his brothers. Later, the people of Israel was enslaved by the Pharaoh.

Abraham's Journey from Ur to Canaan. Painting by József Molnár (1821-1899) that recreates the journey to the Promised Land Prometida.

Judaism

When Abraham sealed the covenant with God in Ur made his way to Canaan, he set the bases for what would be the three great monotheistic religions of the world: Christianity, Islam and Judaism. This latter doctrine dates back 4,000 years.

From Patriarch to one God

Unlike other religions, Judaism has no centralized religious authorities (its religious basis is Abraham's agreement with God), but there are a series of books which, besides describing the Creation, explain the religious, moral, philosophical and even legal precepts with which the Jewish people has legislated its existence.

The Sacred Books

All the sacred books of Judaism are canonical, i.e. they are considered the word of God.

1. **The Torah**
   Also called "doctrine" or Pentateuch, consists of the first five books of the Christian Bible. It was given by God to Moses, and can be interpreted in several ways.
2. **The Talmud**
   Divided into two parts, the *Mishnah* and the *Gemara*, it compiles Jewish rules and numerous theological and philosophical disquisitions on various topics, stories and anecdotes.
3. **Tanakh**
   Known as the Old Testament by Christians, it incorporates the texts of the Torah, the *nevi'im* (Prophets) and *Ketuvim* (writings).

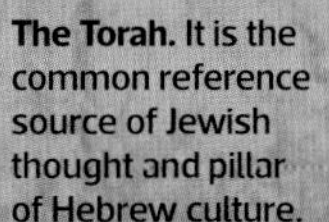

The Torah. It is the common reference source of Jewish thought and pillar of Hebrew culture.

The Prophets

According to tradition, God speaks through His prophets (nevi'im in Hebrew). Beyond this statement, the prophets stand out in the sacred texts as strong critics of power, and they are rebels and rebellious characters.

Jeremiah. Sculpture of the prophet.

ORTHODOXY
According to the Orthodox, in Jewish law one is only Jewish if born of a Jewish mother or if he or she has become so under the supervision of a rabbi.

Origin of Passover

Jews celebrate Passover as a reminder of the biblical exodus, in which they escaped from slavery in Egypt led by Moses (see picture). According to tradition, as they escaped quickly, they baked unleavened bread, and they had to eat that

Precepts. During Passover, food and cooking utensils must have a precise arrangement.

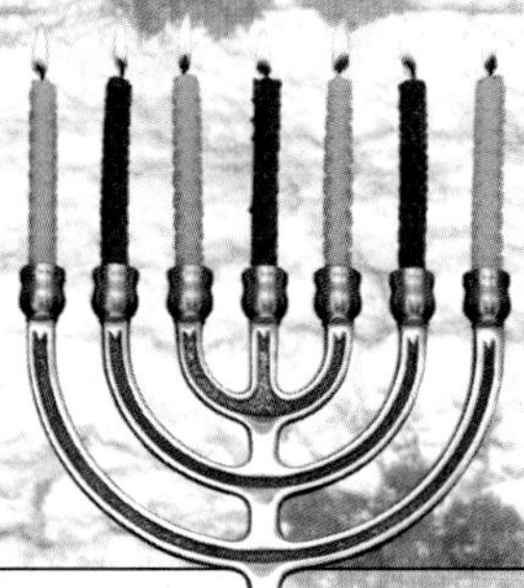

The Pointer or Yad

When religious Jews read the Torah scroll, they do not follow the sequence of the verses with their finger, but with the *yad* (Hebrew for "hand"). It is a small pointer, the end of which is a tiny hand with a pointing finger.

The Menorah

This is a lamp-stand with seven lamps (in Hebrew, *menorah*), under the light of which the religious Jews celebrate the Sabbath, say their prayers and fulfil their religious obligations. It is one of the most iconic Jewish symbols.

The Star of David

The six-pointed star is another identifying symbol of Judaism. *Magen David* in Hebrew means "shield of David," as it was originally identified with the shield used by King David, founder of Jerusalem as the capital of the Jews.

WAILING WALLA
Vestige of the Temple of Jerusalem, this wall is one of the holiest places for Jews.

Chapter 2

Classical Antiquity

The embryonic Chinese Civilization born on the bank of Huang He River became, during the first millennium BC, a solid feudal organization that paved the most powerful and ancient empire in Asia. From the unification of China under the authority of the emperor (third century BC), the prestige of this Empire was born, turned during the Classic Antiquity in an intellectual giant, with a strong commercial activity.

In Europe, immersed in Prehistory until then, Minoan and Mycenaean cultures planted the seeds of the magnificent Classic Greece, mother of western culture. The city-states of Ancient Greece spread their culture widely by establishing trade colonies in the Mediterranean. Their main enemies were the Persians, whose King, Cyrus II the Great, had built a much extensive empire in Central Asia with universal vocation. During its peak, he controlled from India to the western coast of the Mediterranean, surpassing by far the size of any other previous empire.

Greece, however, did not end up at the Persian king's feet, but under the control of Rome, which in the first century managed to rule over the entire basin of the Mediterranean. During that time, and for the first time in a stable manner, commercial routes by land and sea joined Rome with the China of the Han. Distances around the world began to become shorter.

Ancient China

Chinese Civilization developed in a so extensive territory that unifying it turned out to be very complex. For more than two millenniums, the great challenge of the ruling dynasties was to always keep the unity of the Empire.

Annihilation Wars

Having overcome the long period of the legendary dynasties (Xia, Shang and Zhou), China was the first region in the Far East that acquired consciousness of itself. The civil wars held in the first millennium BC, during the Spring and Autumn Period and in the age of the Warring States period, began a process of mutual annihilation among the States of the region, which made unification of China easier for the first time.

Chinaware

Of a great virtuosity, this Chinese invention had a more decorative tan utilitarian character, like this piece form the 18th century. The first examples, made with kaolin or China clay, come from the Shang dynasty (1600-1046 BC).

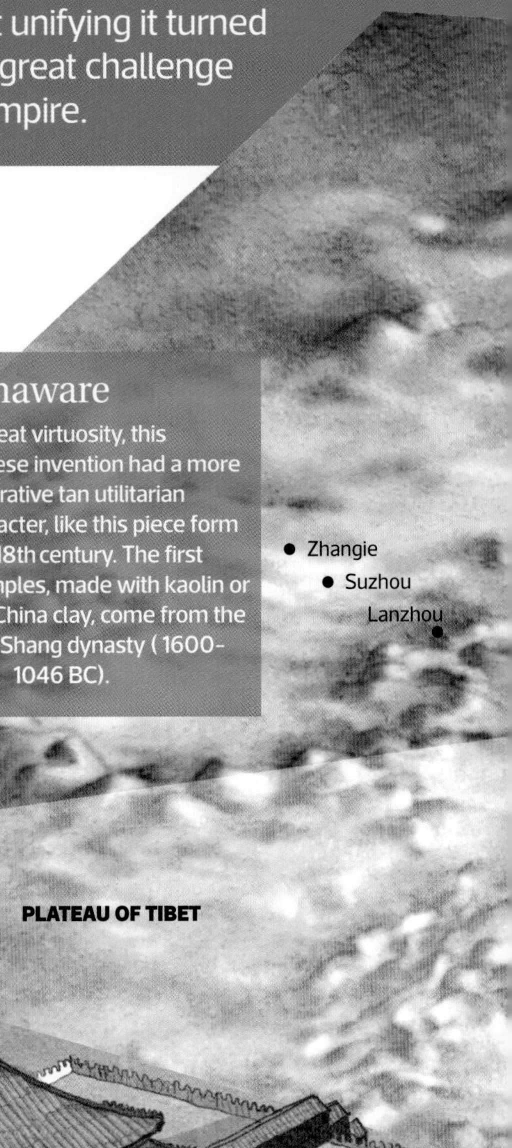

Zhangie

Suzhou

Lanzhou

THE FORBIDDEN CITY

A symbol of imperial power, it is located in the ancient city of Peking. It is dated in the 15th century, and officiated as imperial palace of the Ming and Qing dynasties.

PLATEAU OF TIBET

THE FORBIDDEN CITY

Following Buddha's Steps

Buddhism entered China during the time of the Eastern Hans, in the first century AD, although its real expansion took place in the 5th century. Followers of Buddhism were called *bodhisattva*, a term that makes reference to the search for enlightenment.

MONGOLIA

CHINA

MANCHURIA

GULF OF BO HAI

Xian

Peking

SHANDONG PENINSULA

KOREA

Zhengzhou

Luoyang

Banpo

Xinzbeng

YELLOW SEA

Nanjing

Shanghai

PACIFIC OCEAN

Confucianism

Considered as one of the main figures of Eastern philosophy, Confucius' influence (551 BC - 479 BC) spread to all the spheres of Chinese society. Its ideology is based on the development of human virtues in search for perfection.

Confucius. Statue of the master in the temple dedicated to him in Nanjing.

Dynastic China

History of China is deeply marked by the influence of a series of family clans, later dynasties, which held a great economic and political power, and that lead the destiny of the Empire for more than 2,000 years.

The Chinese Empire Is Born

In the year 221 BC, unification of China was achieved for the first time, ending a period of five centuries of successive feudal wars among family clans. The author of this unification was Ying Zheng, King of Qin, who became the first Chinese emperor with the name of Qin Shi Huang. In 206 BC, Qin dynasty was overthrown by Han dynasty, which ruled for 400 years and established Confucianism as the official ideology. At the end of the Han period, in the year 220, the country divided again and it would not be until the government of Sui dynasty (581-618) when China was reunified.

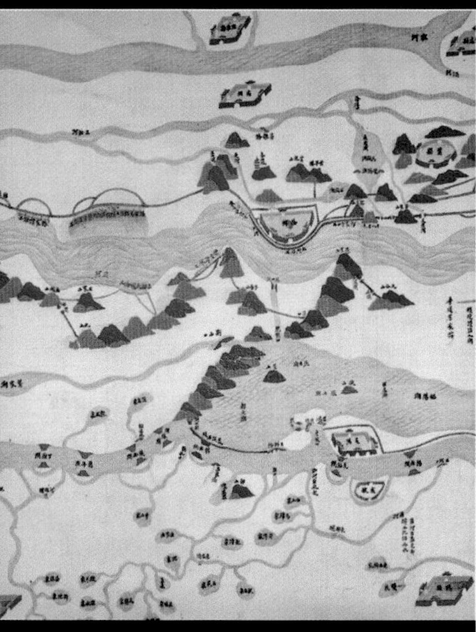

Great Channel. Detailed map from the 18th century of the route of the enormous artificial channel started by the Sui dynasty.

Artificial Channel

Emperor Yang Guang, of Sui dynasty (581-618) around 604, ordered to build a channel that would join the cities of Peking, in the north, and Hangzhou, in the south. Under the ruling of the Sui, the work reached 1,700 km. In length, and during the Tang dynasty (618–907), it was able to be widely used for transporting merchandise.

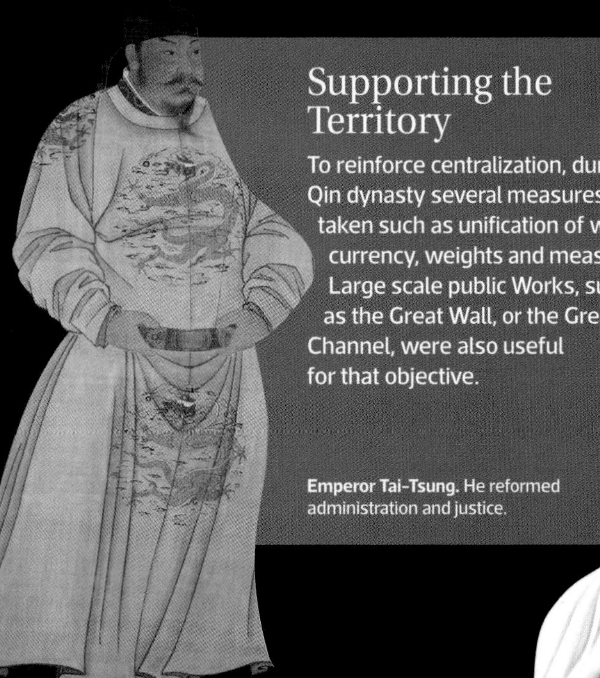

Supporting the Territory

To reinforce centralization, during the Qin dynasty several measures were taken such as unification of writing, currency, weights and measures. Large scale public Works, such as the Great Wall, or the Great Channel, were also useful for that objective.

Emperor Tai-Tsung. He reformed administration and justice.

SPREADING OF BUDDHISM

During Tang dynasty, Buddhism became a central aspect of Chinese life and culture. In the image, a statuette of Buddha from the 13th or 14th century.

The Silk Road

Despite geographical fragmentation and the constant confrontations, Han period was of a great economic prosperity. The Silk Road was one of its inheritances.

Chinaware and the Dynasties

Chinaware developed artistically during the dynastic periods. In each one of them, it was characterized by different shapes, enamels and motifs. With the passing of time it became an important exportation item, although the best pieces were destined for the imperial palace.

Ming Chinaware. Polychromatic base of the 15th century.

The Classic Empire

Han dynasty, the one of longest duration in Chinese history, had the leading role in what is considered the great Classic Chinese Empire. In the Han period (206 BC-220) order was reestablished and feudalism was reintroduced, the political function was democratized and Confucianism recovered belief. After the Han dynasty there were several barbarian dynasties, and later the long periods of Tang, Song, Ming and Qing dynasties.

The Child-Emperor

The last Chinese imperial dynasty was Manchu or Qing (1644-1912), and its last emperor, Xuantong V. Born on February 2nd, 1906, he was appointed emperor at the age of three years. He died in 1967.

BRONZE
Ancient dynasties like Shang and Zhou stood out for the dexterity in working with bronze.

The Emperor and His Court

Heir and divine representative on Earth, the power of the emperor of China was absolute in political, social, religious, economic and cultural life of his subjects. To the title of Emperor, they added "Son of the Sky."

Divine Power

Even thought the emperor was the personification of power itself in Ancient China, there were rulers who accompanied their authority with an efficient and hierarchical court that counted with the main administrative public servants and military. Other emperors, on the other hand, practiced a despotic authority, hardly supported by a small entourage.

EMPEROR
Highest figure of the social Chinese hierarchy, even the most eminent public servants and priests owed him total submission.

SERVANTS
They surrounded the emperor and his family. They had an extensive chores hierarchy, and if they did not fulfill them, they could pay with their lives.

Everyday Life

In the emperor's court, life was ruled by a complex framework of strict codes that regulated the public and the private, family bonds, relationship among servants and even treatment of domestic animals.

SCRIBES
They were particularly respected for their knowledge of writing and reading. There was always one next to the emperor.

Fisherman. In the image, statue found in a tomb of Han dynasty.

Women of the Court

The role of women of the court with respect to men was as submissive as the one of the rest. Among their duties was the making of the silk used by the ruling class. On the right, a detail of the *Ladies of the court preparing silk cloths for emperor Hui Tsung*, from the 12th century.

EXCLUSIVITY
Silk was already being made in China more than four millenniums ago.

EMPRESS
She did not practice any government functions. Also, the emperor had the right to practice polygamy.

ROYAL CHAMBERS
They were very luxurious environments, elegantly decorated with statues from Chinese culture.

PRESENCE
Numerous people always surrounded the emperor so his person stood out among the crowd.

MAGISTRATES.
They made up state bureaucracy. They enforced laws, collected taxes, dictated justice and made census.

Only One Queen

Of royal descent, Wu Zetian married emperor Gaozong. After her husband's death, she ruled through her sons, Zhongzong and Ruizong, to finally proclaim herself empress. She was the only one to rule as queen in imperial China.

Wu Zetian.
Ruled from 625 to 705.

Ancient Greece

Between the 8th and 5th centuries BC, Greek Civilization expanded throughout the Mediterranean by establishing commercial colonies. Ancient Greek opened the route to democracy, revolutionized arts and thought, and invented sports.

The Greek World

Greek Civilization was characterized by a great political fragmentation, even though its city-states (poleis) shared the same language and culture. The rugged landscape of the Peloponnese contributed to this isolation of the poleis that formed the Greek world. Sparta and especially Athens were the most powerful ones. This later one reached political and cultural heights previously unknown.

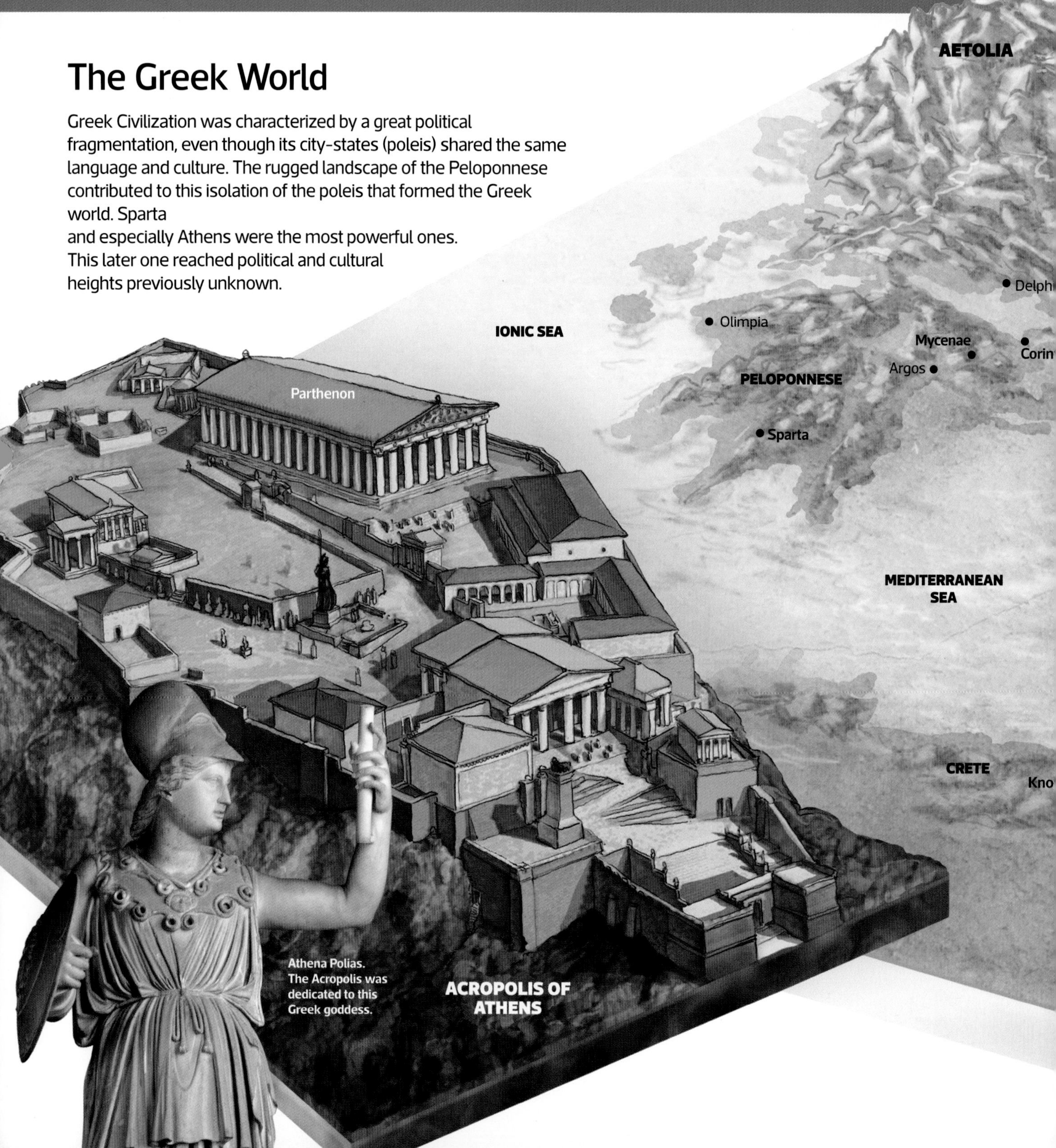

Athena Polias. The Acropolis was dedicated to this Greek goddess.

The Age of Pericles

During the 5th century BC, Athens, ruled by Pericles (in the image), lived its peak. Under this ruler, the city shone in such a way in the cultural and political field that the period is known as the Age of Pericles.

The Greek Epic Stories

Due to their narrative and aesthetics, the *Odyssey and the Iliad*, attributed to Greek poet Homer, constitute the origin of western literature.

Homer. He lived in the 9th-8th centuries BC, if he really existed.

Symbol of Power

Athens tried to show its leadership in the Greek world with the Acropolis. Its main temple, the Parthenon, dates from year 438 BC. The Acropolis was finished towards the year 406 BC, with the construction of the Erechtheion (to the right with its Caryatid characteristics), which symbolize reconciliation with divinities that disputed the city: Athens and Poseidon.

The Greek Poleis

After the fall of Mycenaean Civilization in the 12th century BC Greeks divided in small communities that four centuries later, had transformed into city-states. The poleis were independent and each one had its own traits.

Towards Democracy

In their beginning, Greek poleis were ruled by military leaders (basileus). Beginning on the 7th century BC these were displaced by oligarchic governments. With time, the aristocracy regime, which had already suffered the so called era of tyrannies (was replaced by democracy, whose highest development took place in Athens in the 5th century BC).

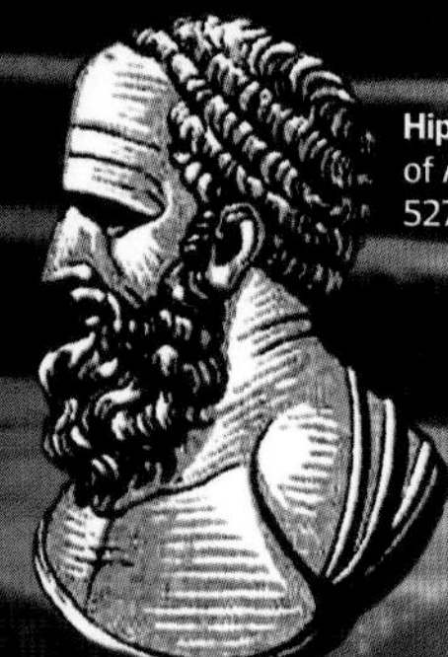

Hipparchus. Tyrant of Athens between 527 and 514 BC.

The tyrants

The era of tyrants in Greece lasted during the 6th century BC until the 5th century BC, The tyrants had Access to power mostly thanks to popular support. They were born in a moment of transit towards democracy, when aristocracy had begun to weaken.

Solon

Born in Athens in the year 640 BC, Solon (in the image) was elected Archon, title that designated the main magistrates in the Greek poleis. A short time after being appointed, he issued a constitution that established the basis of Athenian democracy. He divided Athenians in four classes of citizens, according to their wealth and not for their birth. With this disposition, he weakened the power of nobility, emerged around the figure of the basileus, which had a hereditary status. He died in Cyprus in 558 BC.

Ostracon. Athenian citizens used pieces of pottery to vote.

Kameiros. City of the island of Rhodes, in the Aegean Sea, stood out for its walled acropolis and its temples.

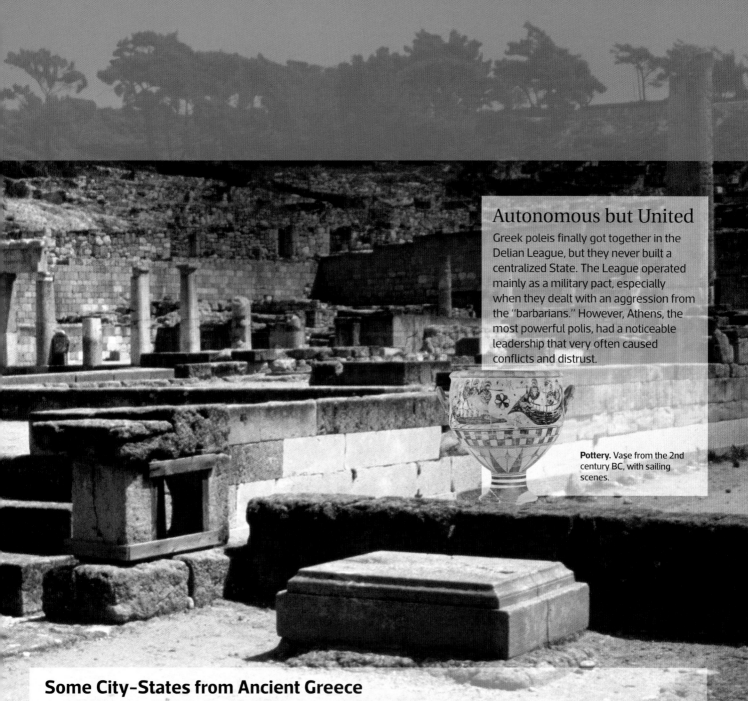

Autonomous but United

Greek poleis finally got together in the Delian League, but they never built a centralized State. The League operated mainly as a military pact, especially when they dealt with an aggression from the "barbarians." However, Athens, the most powerful polis, had a noticeable leadership that very often caused conflicts and distrust.

Pottery. Vase from the 2nd century BC, with sailing scenes.

Some City-States from Ancient Greece

1 Aegina
Located in the island in front of Athens, it was always in conflict with the capital of Attica. In 431 BC Athenians proceeded to depopulate it.

2 Megara
It constantly competed with its neighbor Athens. It reached great prosperity in the 7th century BC and established several colonies in the Black Sea region.

3 Mileto
Founded by Ionians, it became an important colonizing center in the 8th century BC. It was the homeland of prominent wise men such as Thales and Hecataeus.

4 Ephesus
Founded around 1,000 BC, it became a great commercial center. Its Temple of Artemis or Artemision, today in ruins, was one of the seven wonders of the world.

Greek Cultural Heritage

Philosophy as a system of thought, and poetry and theater as literary manifestation were born in Classic Greece, and together with the development of the rest of the arts and sciences, they are essential to understand the current western culture.

A Larger Creative Freedom

Classic Greece society enjoyed more freedom of thought and expression than in previous eras. This way, it was able to shape a more modern way of thinking, which became visible in arts and sciences: architecture and sculpture adopted rules where proportion and harmony were synonyms of beauty; philosophy left aside the magical explanations to begin using reason.

THE PARTHENON
This famous Doric style marble temple has been used as model of many later buildings.

Sculpture

The *Discobolus* or discus thrower, work of Myron, shows the moment in which the athlete balances the disc, just about to throw it. This action reflects a change in the concept of art, which aims to perpetuate the moment of movement, in contrast with the rigidity of archaic statues.

Discobolus. Roman copy in marble of the renowned sculpture from the 5th century BC by Myron of Eleutherae.

Philosophy

Socrates, Plato and Aristotle (in the image) are the three great thinkers of classic Greek philosophy. They tried to answer the questions the human existence suggest, from the most elementary to the most complex, through observation and speculative thinking.

SOPHOCLES
He was one of the great tragic poets along with Euripides and Aeschylus. Only seven of his Works are preserved, among them *Electra*, *Antigone* and *Oedipus* the King.

Literary Creation

Literature as an art appeared in Ancient Greece. Poets Homer and Hesiod reproduced ancient myths and displayed all the narrative elements of epic, beginning this way the artistic development of Word. In combination with epic, they gave place to drama, one of the most complex literary expressions.

Theater

Greeks established the theatrical architecture model whose basic features, perfected by Romans, are still current: a building dedicated solely to scenic representations, whose architectural organization clearly separates the space for the audience from the one reserved for performance.

Theater of Epidaurus. Built with Stone in the 4th century BC. It is believed that the first theaters were made with wood.

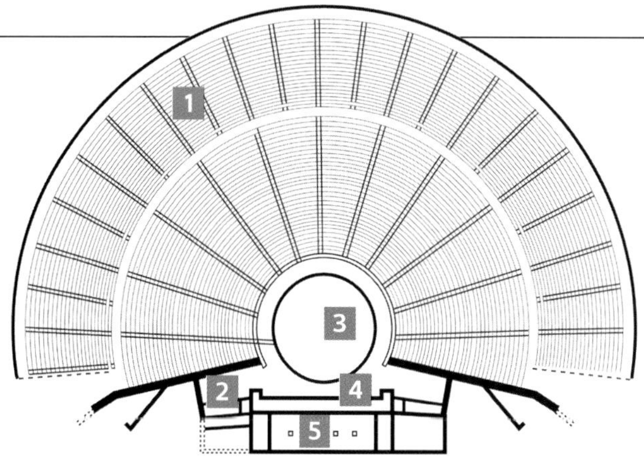

1 Cavea Seating sections for the audience
2 Parodus Side entrance to the theater
3 Orchestra Circular space reserved for the chorus
4 Proscenium Stage area for actors
5 Scene Space for decorations and wardrobe

Architectural Orders

DORIC
- **Origin:** Continental Greece
- **Appearance:** 7th century BC
- **Column:** with simple base and capital, with one spherical section and another one square.

IONIC
- **Origin:** Ionian Islands
- **Appearance:** 6th century BC
- **Column:** base and capital with two volutes under the abacus, which delimit a convex moulding of ovas.

CORINTHIAN
- **Origin:** Athens
- **Appearance:** 5 century BC
- **Column:** with base and capital with the shape of an inverted bell, decorated with acanthus leaves.

The Persian Empire

The territory conquered by the Persians between the 6th and 4th centuries BC was so extended that the kingdom earned the name of Universal Empire. Its borders increased or reduced according to administrative and politic efficiency of the rulers.

The World as a Limit

Supported by an exceptional war machine and lead by the ambitious Achaemenid dynasty, the Persian empire was organized for confrontation and subjugating its adversaries, to whom it imposed heavy taxes to maintain its structure and its conquest objectives. Appearing in the large Iranian plateaus, it managed to rule from the Mediterranean coast to India and Egypt, subjugating people and regions as wide as different. Its main kings were Cyrus II the Great and Darius I.

PERSIAN EMPIRE

BLACK SEA

MACEDONIA

Sardis

GREECE

MONUMENTAL CITY
It was one of the four capitals of the empire. It had great palaces. It was completed along several kingdoms.

Diversity

History of the Persian empire of the Achaemenids is rich in cultural Exchange. From Egypt to beyond the Caspian Sea and the Persian Gulf, incorporation of traditions from the people that formed it was one of its main characteristics.

Nabataean woman. Persian portrait carved in stone.

POTTERY
One of the first artistic expressions of the ancient Persian empire was pottery (in the image, statue of a deity).

Mazdaism

Tolerant with the different worships of the religions they had conquered, Persians adopted Mazdeism as their official religion. Much later, in the 8th century with the Muslim conquest, Islamism would end up establishing itself as Persian official and State religion.

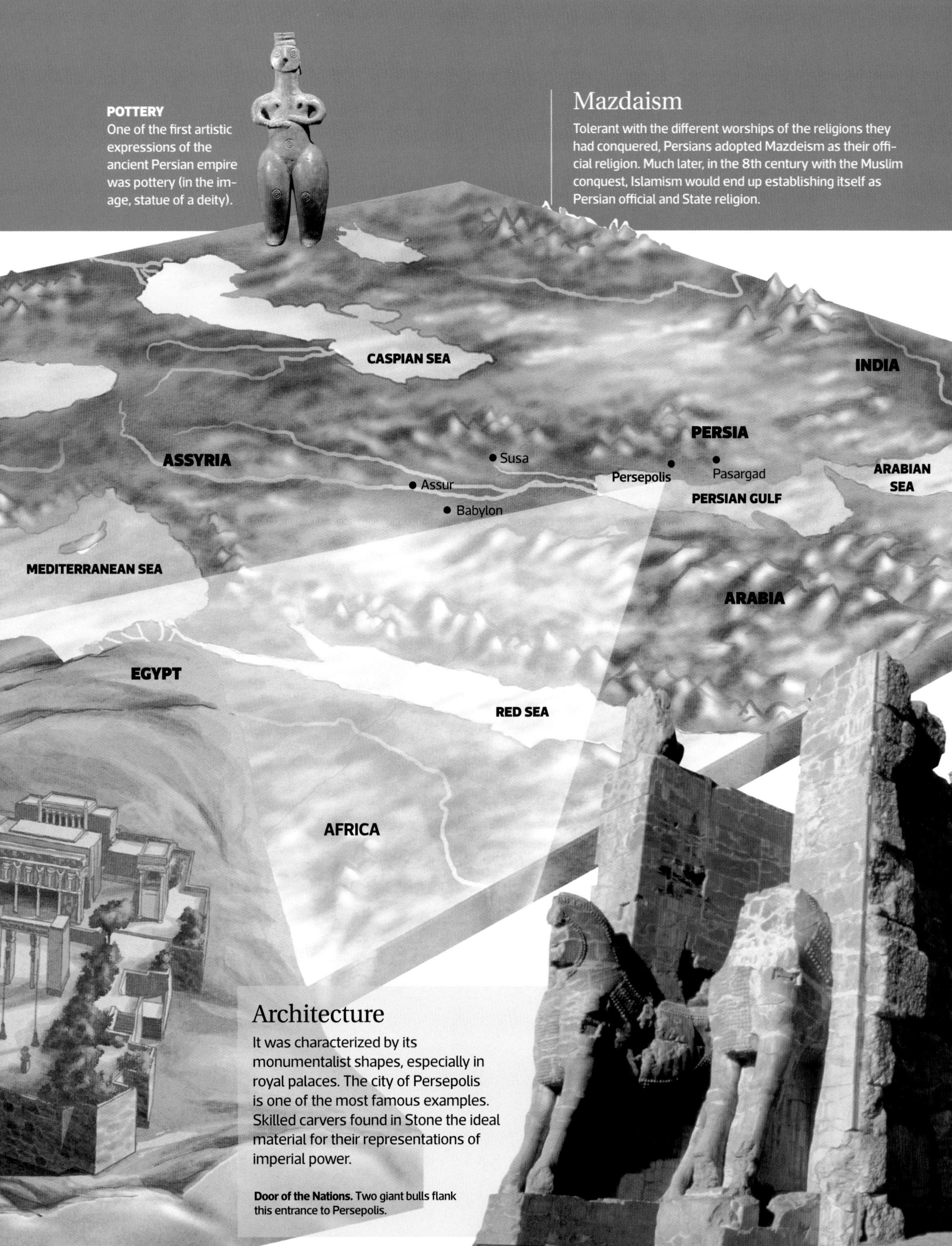

Architecture

It was characterized by its monumentalist shapes, especially in royal palaces. The city of Persepolis is one of the most famous examples. Skilled carvers found in Stone the ideal material for their representations of imperial power.

Door of the Nations. Two giant bulls flank this entrance to Persepolis.

Cyrus, the Founder of the Empire

Forger of the most powerful empire of its time, Median-Persian King Cyrus II the Great was notable for his incessant conquering activity. He entered history for extending the limits of the Achaemenid Empire to the Mediterranean coast and the Indus River.

A Glorious Reign

In the year 559 BC Cyrus, son of the governor of a region in the Median Empire, rose up against King Astyages and managed to get control of Ecbatana, Median capital in those years. Considered as the founder of the Persian Empire, Cyrus (who entered history as Cyrus II the Great) expanded the domain of his kingdom until it reached eight million square kilometers. This King stood out for allowing a high level of autonomy to the conquered cities.

BABYLONIAN MODEL Persians enriched the decoration on lacquered bricks used by Babylonians.

The Conquests

Cyrus II started the expansion of the Median-Persian kingdom with the subjugation of Lydia and the Ionic coastal cities. After dominating the entire Asia minor, he defeated the New Babylonians and ended the exile of the Jews (in the image, the battle for Jerusalem). He rapidly expanded the Empire to the Indus River. His great defeat was against the Massagetae, where he lost his life. He was succeeded by his son Cambyses, who annexed Egypt for him.

Queen Tomyris

According to Greek historian Herodotus, after the failure of Cyrus II to marry Tomyris (queen of the Massagetae, nomad people from the east of Asia), the Persian King confronted her in battle. Cyrus managed to capture the firstborn son of queen and made him commit suicide. Tomyris decide to take revenge and, after defeating Cyrus in a new battle, she had him beheaded.

Death of Cyrus. Tomyris holds the head of King Cyrus II in this painting of the 17th century by Luca Ferrari.

Achaemenid Art

Persians were known for the excellent quality of their bas-relief Works, and also for their pottery and the sculptures dedicated to their kings, craved on the sides of mountains or in tombs, and in their imperial palaces.

CYRUS' TOMB
It was built in Pasargard, city of origin of the Achaemenid dynasty. Inspired on the Mesopotamian ziggurats, it rises over large blocks of stones.

King of Asia

Born in 590–580 BC, Cyrus II needed only half a century of life to become "King of Asia," due to the conquering efficiency of his empire.

Persepolis, the Persian Capital

Built by King Darius, it became the capital of the Empire towards the year 520 BC. His son Xerxes I and his grandson Artaxerxes I finished some of the edifications. The main function of this architectural jewel of Achaemenid architecture was serving as ceremonial center.

Sporadic Use

Persepolis was located in the south east of Persia, in a plateau with a surface of around 10 hectares. The city was occupied only once a year, during the New Year ceremonies, when rulers from all around the Empire took their tribute to the King. Reconstruction of the city, very dilapidated due to the passing of time, was possible thanks to Charles Chipiez and Georges Perrot, who at the end of the 19th century had written down the architectural details and the used material in its construction.

PALACE OF THE HUNDRED COLUMNS
Also known as Hall of the Throne, the building measured 70 m on each side. It was surrounded by 36 columns in six rows.

PROTECTION
Its defense system made Persepolis a practically unbeatable.

Tributes to the King

In the bas-relieves of Persepolis there we can see scenes that show the submission of the subjects from conquered kingdoms to the Persian King, offering their presents to him.

Bas-relief. Detail of the dignitaries' parade on a wall in Persepolis.

HOLLOW WALLS
It has been discovered that the walls made of large bricks were hollow, and that they were framed with stone.

Remodeling of Darius the Great

King Darius restructured the gigantic Persian Empire creating 23 satrapies or provinces, juridically equal, in whose front he placed Persian rulers. He also built en extensive network of roads for the royal mailmen, and reformed the army, turning it into a more effective weapon for conquest. The daric was established as the only currency of the Empire.

ROYAL GUARD
Bas-relief of the 5th century BC that shows the guards with spears and shields.

TREASURE
Here is where the riches that the Persian Empire accumulated in its regular conquests were stored.

APADANA
Used by the King as a hearing hall, this building was, together with the Palace of Thousand Columns, the most important one in the city.

DOOR OF THE NATIONS
It was one of the main accesses to the city. Its design is inspired in Assyrian architectural shapes. On each side they had a sculpture of a bull 5,5 m. high.

Recreation. Illustration of the city of Persepolis in the era of King Darius, from the drawings of Charles Chipiez.

The Celts

Celts were the first ones to settle in Europe during the Iron Age. Towards the 5th century BC, they began to form a singular culture, a conglomerate of tribes that shared the same language and culture: the Tène Civilization.

Expansion to the West

Extraordinary goldsmiths and jewelers, travelers, farmers and warriors, Celts adapted to the most diverse geographies, they managed to dominate central Europe, and they extended their influence from Wales to Ireland, where their power lasted for longer time, to the Black Sea. They withstood initially against Rome, although the Gallic (Roman name for Celts) would fall to Julius Caesar centuries later.

Paganism

They were a superstitious nation, who adored divinities related with nature and held ceremonies and rituals (among these, human sacrifices). They showed reverential respect for the large granite blocks that they found in their territory, since they believed they had been taken there by very powerful people. They carved their own inscriptions on these same stones.

Marks. They used to decorate stones and swords with geometric or linear drawings.

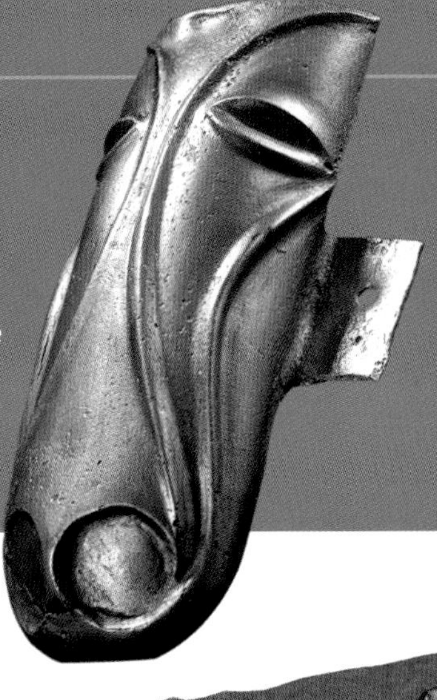

MASK
Bronze piece from the 1st century, made by the Briganti people, settled in the British Islands.

Independent Tribes

Celts were a group of clans that behaved in an autonomous way, even though they had occasional alliances. Heavily armed, they colonized regions of Central and Western Europe in the 5th to 3th centuries BC. Sometimes they mixed with aborigines, as it happened in Iberia with the Celtiberians or in the Russian steppes with the Celtischythians.

HALLSTATT

THE VILLAGES
Celts grouped together in walled fortresses, sheltered by natural protections. In general, they did not keep a planned urban line.

BLACK SEA

GALATIA

Celt Goldsmithing

Celt tribes made a large variety of objects that show how important personal ostentation was for them, such as brooches, necklaces, earrings, collars and rings. They also went to a lot of effort in the decoration of their weapons, especially the ornamental richness of sword handles and shields. Bronze was the main raw material used.

Shield. Made in bronze, in the 2nd to 1st centuries BC.

Celtic Dwellings

Everyday life of the Celtic tribes, which lived scattered in independent villages, developed mainly inside their walls. It was not until the 2nd century BC when Celts started to build new cities, once their expansion phase in Europe was finished.

Organization

Originally, Celtic towns were characterized for the cylindrical shape of their houses. But near the 1st century BC, when the influence of the Roman culture began to leave a mark, they started building houses with square or rectangular floors. Houses only had one kind of ambience, they grouped families and were built near natural defenses or walls to protect them from enemies and harsh weather.

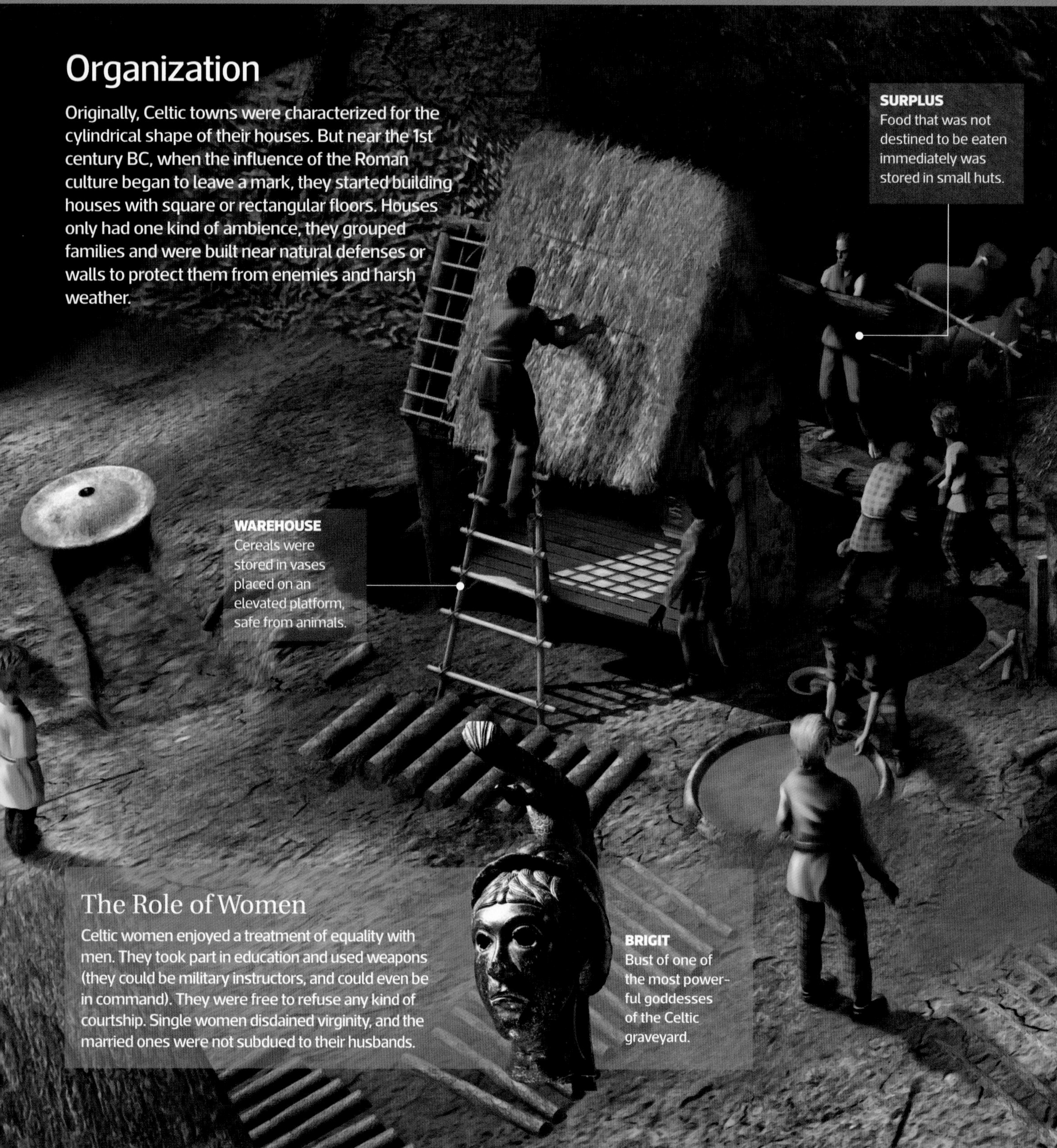

SURPLUS
Food that was not destined to be eaten immediately was stored in small huts.

WAREHOUSE
Cereals were stored in vases placed on an elevated platform, safe from animals.

The Role of Women

Celtic women enjoyed a treatment of equality with men. They took part in education and used weapons (they could be military instructors, and could even be in command). They were free to refuse any kind of courtship. Single women disdained virginity, and the married ones were not subdued to their husbands.

BRIGIT
Bust of one of the most powerful goddesses of the Celtic graveyard.

ORNAMENTS
Celts used to wear a dark wool cape open on one side and closed with a brooch. Men adorned themselves with torques and metal brooches (like the ones in the image) and women with necklaces, bracelets and small bells.

THE ROOFS
With a gable roof or with a cylindrical shape, they were built with a wooden frame covered with straw and clay.

FIRE
Essential for cooking and for heating the home, it burned in the center of the house, inside a circle made with stones.

ANIMALS
Horses, pigs and sheep wandered around the houses. They were of upmost importance for the economy of the tribes.

THE FLOOR
The terrain was covered with a first layer of thin stone to level it, and over it, another one of rammed clay.

THE WALLS
Even though materials varied according to the region, they usually used some kind of wicker covered with clay to obtain strength.

The Splendor of Rome

Beginning with a handful of Etruscan city-states of the Lazio region, lead by Rome, a political, military and economic entity began to grow, and in time, it became one of the most powerful kingdoms of Antiquity.

The Building of the Empire

After its first steps under monarchy (753-509 BC), demands for the participation and social equality contributed to the Republic. Fights of classes between patricians and plebeians marked the republican stage until the beginning of the 3rd century BC, without this being an obstacle for Rome to complete in this same era its domain of the Italian Peninsula and to begin the conquest of the entire Mediterranean. In the year 27 BC, after long civil wars, Octavius Augustus founded the Roman Empire.

THE CIRCUS
To entertain the masses, ampitheaters were built where there were chariot races and gladiators combats. The Coliseum had a capacity of 50,000 people.

Division of the Empire

Constantine's reign marked a crucial moment of the glory of Rome, but also a decisive change in direction. The capital was moved to Constantinople (current Istanbul), better protected from the harassment of "barbarians." The price ended up being the division of the Empire in two parts: the Western Roman Empire and the Eastern Roman Empire.

ARCH OF CONSTANTINE
Finished in the year 315, this arch commemorates the victory of Constantine I the Great in the Battle of Milvian Bridge.

venna
ADRIATIC SEA
TRURIA
LAZIO
SAMNIUM
Taranto
Rome
Pompey
IONIC SEA
SICILY
Syracuse
TYRRHENIAN SEA
SARDINIA

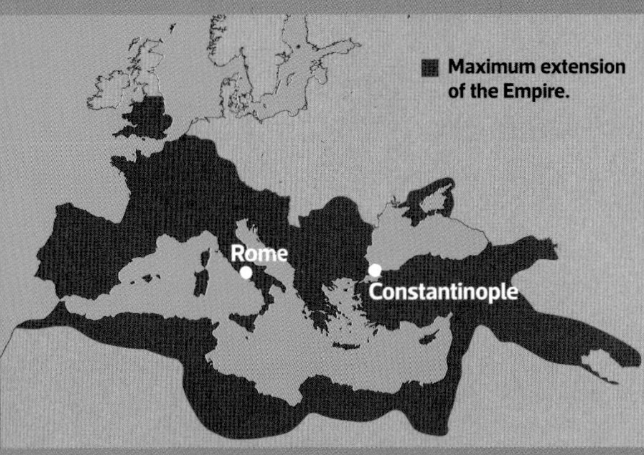

THE ROMAN EMPIRE UNDER THE REIGN OF TRAJAN
With Trajan, the Empire reached its maximum extension. The strategic position of the Italian Peninsula in the Mediterranean made the supremacy of Rome easier on both sides of this sea, to a point in which Romans baptized it as Mare Nostrum ("Our Sea").

REMAINS
Almost all Europe and part of Eastern Asia and North of Africa fell under the domain of a Roman Civilization that left deep tracks in universal culture.

Porta Nigra. In Tier (Germany).

The Roman Senate

During the monarchic period of Rome, the *Senatus* (Assembly of Elders) was created as a counterweight of the royal power. The first senators, with a lifelong position, were appointed by the family clans (*gens*). The institution adapted later to the Republic and to the Empire.

An Advisory Body

The Senate had, as its main function, advising the King in State issues. This function was done on the king's request, and through the *senatus consulto* (senatorial consultations). Very often, the King had the deference of submitting to voting by the Senate his decisions, a way to accept and capitalize the social prestige that senators had. The Senate was also temporarily in charge of the government in the absence or death of the King.

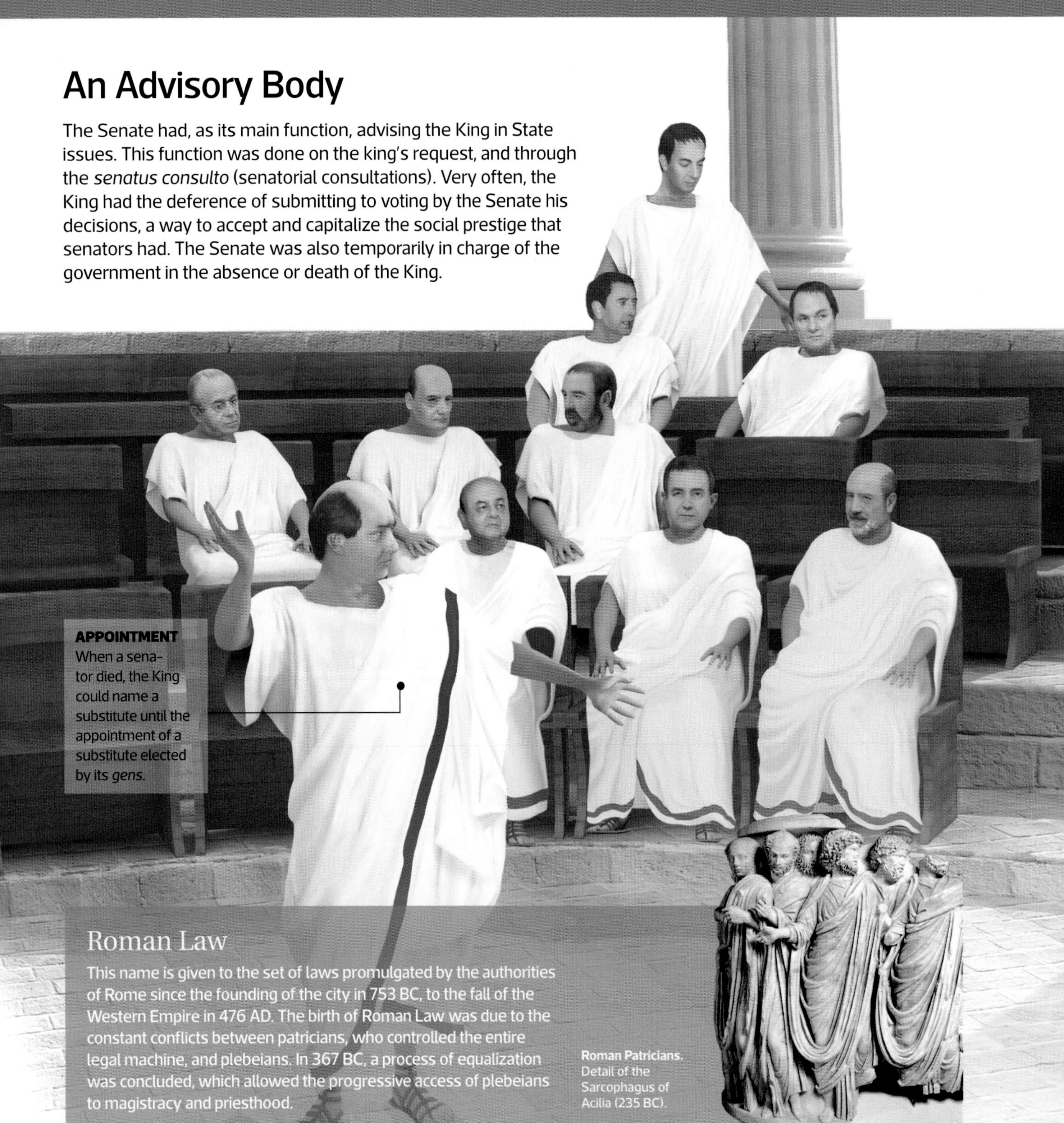

APPOINTMENT
When a senator died, the King could name a substitute until the appointment of a substitute elected by its *gens*.

Roman Law

This name is given to the set of laws promulgated by the authorities of Rome since the founding of the city in 753 BC, to the fall of the Western Empire in 476 AD. The birth of Roman Law was due to the constant conflicts between patricians, who controlled the entire legal machine, and plebeians. In 367 BC, a process of equalization was concluded, which allowed the progressive access of plebeians to magistracy and priesthood.

Roman Patricians. Detail of the Sarcophagus of Acilia (235 BC).

The Code of Justinian

Emperor of Byzantium between 527 and 565, Justinian ordered to compile the Roman laws. His *Corpus Iuris Civilis* became the first source for the knowledge of Roman Law and inspired most of the following legislative compendiums.

JUSTINIAN I
Portrait of the emperor, one of the most important personalities in his time, in a Byzantine coin.

Inequality

Differences between plebeians and patricians were maintained, although the plebeians could now be senators. For example, prohibition to marry with a member of a different social class was still maintained.

ROMAN FASCES
Of Etruscan origin, this cylinder was made with 30 wooden rods (one for each Roman Curia), tied with a ribbon.

Figures of the Senate

Tribunes
Of a plebeian origin, tribunes could attend the Senate meetings and present motions, although they did not have the right to vote.

Lictors
They accompanied the senators and were in charge of enforcing the law on site. For this, they used to carry some wooden rods that held a *labrys*: the fasces.

Censors
A figure created by patrician nobility, to its initial function on census and on the budget, the appointment of vacancies in the Senate was added.

CONTROL
In time, the Senate took control of all political decisions, administration, division of public land, and even the public treasure.

Constitutional Reforms

Among the great Roman legislative reformists, in the 4th century BC Appius Claudius stands out (in the image on the right), who proposed the inclusion of the sons of the liberated in the Senate. This indicates the increasing power of tradesmen and artisans. But there was a big rejection from the patricians.

Chapter 3

Civilizations of the Medieval Period

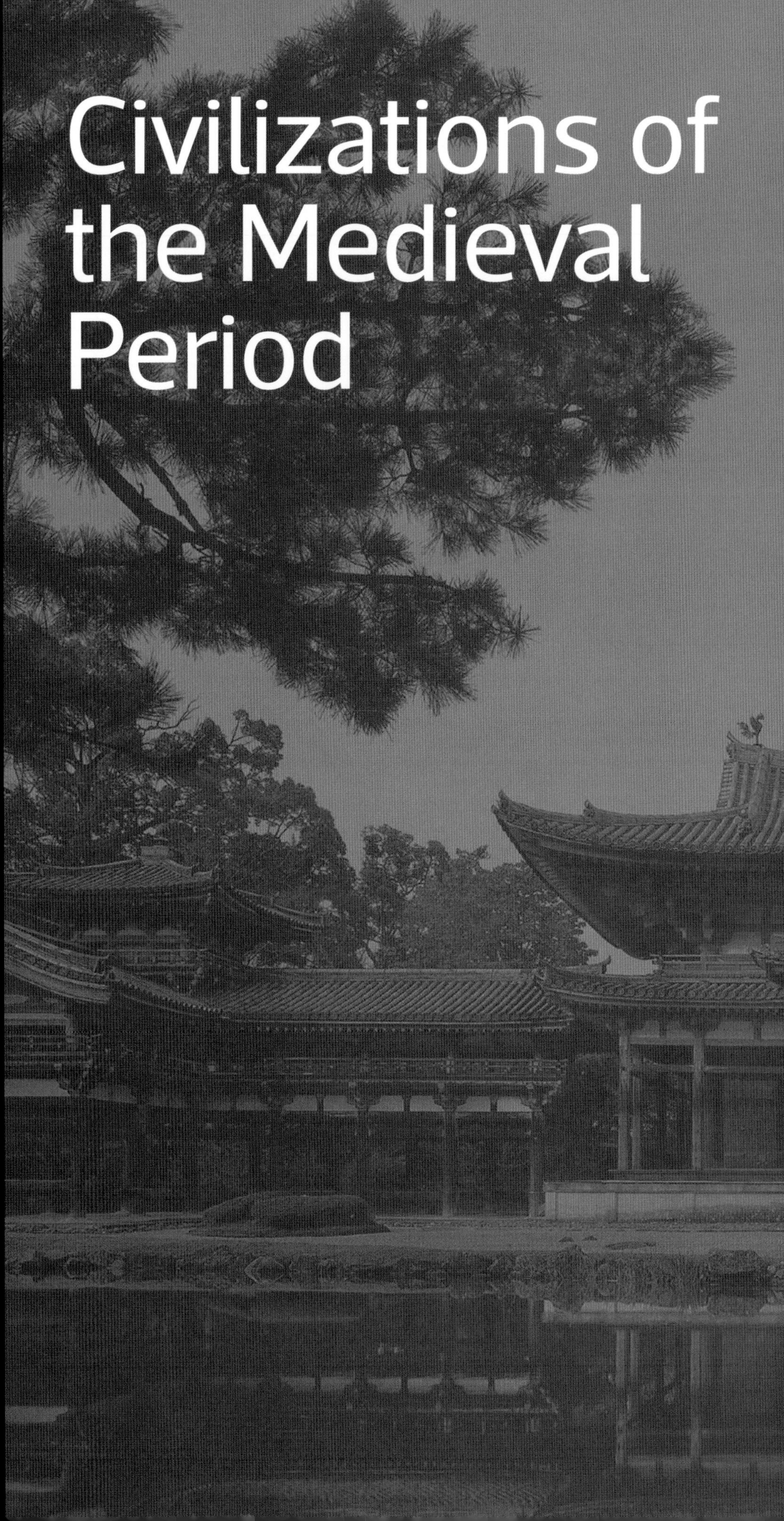

With the fall of the Roman Empire and its separation, Europe entered the Middle Ages. While the western part of the Empire was declining rapidly, the eastern part (the new Byzantine Empire, with capital in Constantinople) secured itself as a power, and preserved the Greek-Roman legacy.

EIn Arabia, around the figure of Mohammed and his unprecedented cult, Islam, in the 7th century a brand new kingdom arose, who found no barriers to its rapid expansion in the north of Africa, until reaching the Iberia peninsula and India. Islamic Empire left a profound cultural legacy despite the political fragmentation which characterized it.

With a much more local profile, in the Far East Japan, a new empire had constituted itself since the 4th century, consolidating a feudal regime of clans, which would stay current until the 19th century.

Meanwhile, from the north of Europe, Vikings had begun their pillaging raids, and their maritime expeditions in the Atlantic, the Baltic and the Mediterranean Sea, which lead them to be the first Europeans to set foot in America. In this continent, the Mayas, the Aztecs and the Incas capitalized the inheritance of the first American cultures and built impressive cities in Mesoamerica and in the Central Andes, reaching a high level of complexity in their state organizations.

The Vikings

Great sailors and warriors, Vikings did not form homogeneous Civilization and culture. These people from the north of Europe terrified the rest of the continent with their raids. They were brilliant in maritime exploration and they mastered the metallurgical technique.

The Viking Era

Natives from Scandinavia, Vikings began to earn their fame as violent people towards the end of the 7th century, when in the year 793 they attacked and destroyed Lindisfarne monastery, located in the coast of England. This date is considered as the beginning of the Viking Era. Since then, and for the next three centuries, they swept their feared weapons from the British coast to the western part of current Russia.

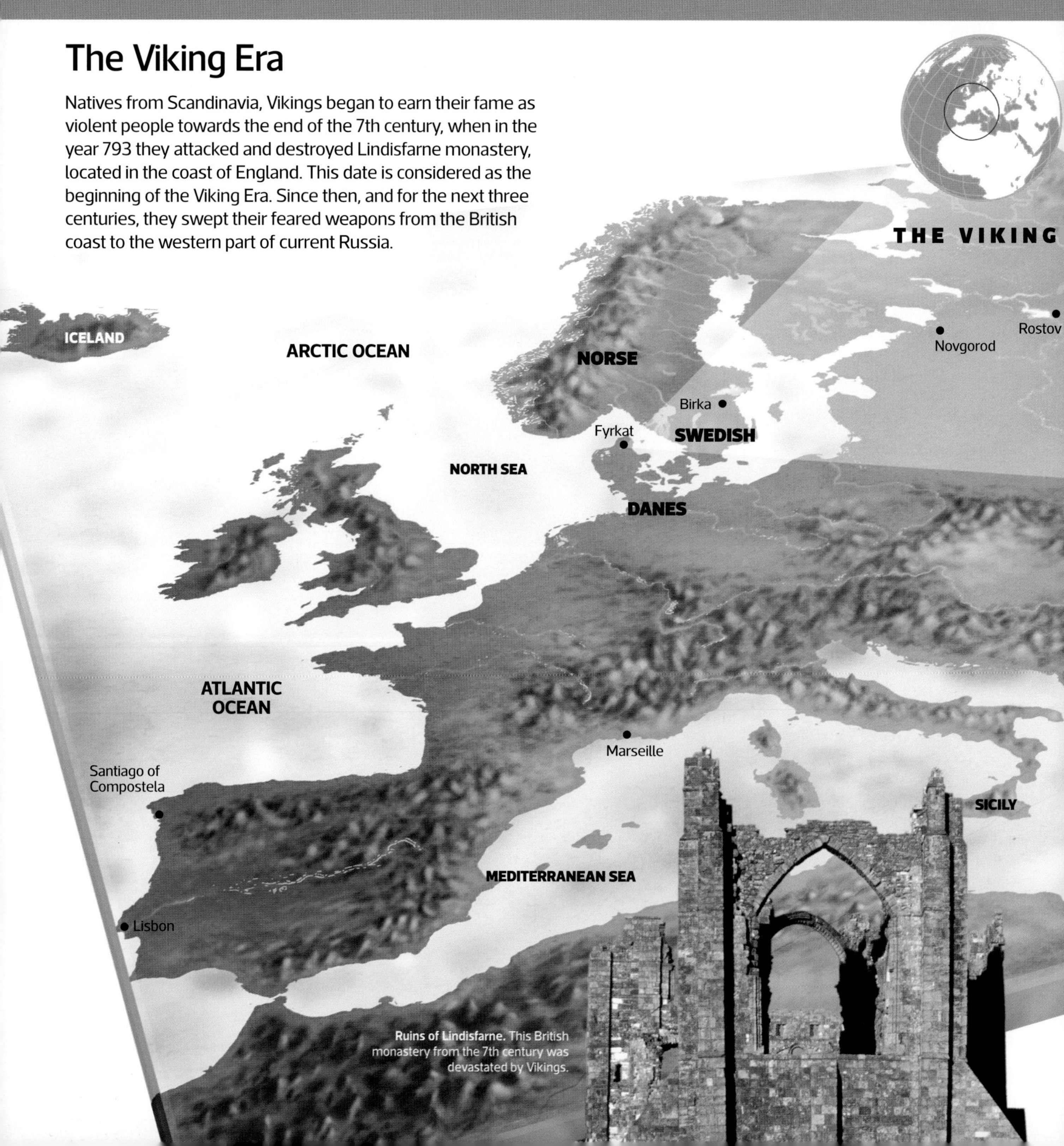

Ruins of Lindisfarne. This British monastery from the 7th century was devastated by Vikings.

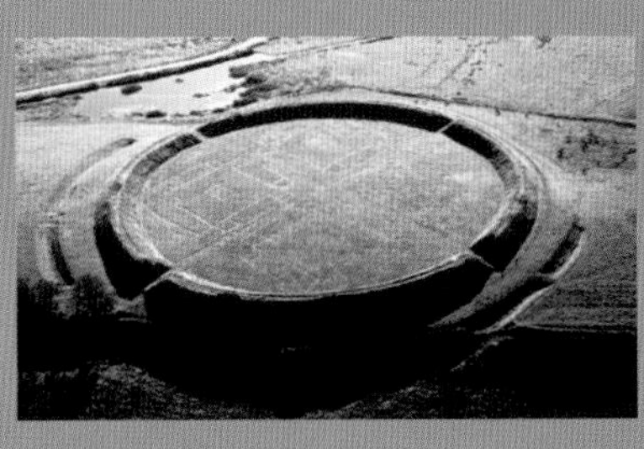

Settlements

Viking people (with their own differences) lived in fortified settlements in which they built constructions similar to barracks. Some of these buildings were used as housing, but others served as warehouses, stables and workshops. On the left, an aerial view of the ruins of Danish fortress of Fyrkat.

FORTRESS
In Denmark, Vikings built circular fortresses protected by a wall of earth and a moat.

Kiev

BLACK SEA

Constantinople

Stone of Karlevi. Located in the Baltic island of Oland, it is from the 11th century. It contains the most ancient Skaldic verse ever known.

Runes

Scandinavian people used different runic alphabets, which share some letters called runes. This writing system, although basic, allowed establishing judicial edicts and sentences, and to narrate stories of dynastic successions and battles. Thanks to the runic stones found in the north of Europe, part of Viking history was able to be reconstructed.

WARRIOR'S HELMET
Above, a helmet belonging to Vendel culture, in current Swe-den, considered as pre-Viking.

Viking Explorers

Since the last years of the 8th century to the 9th, the warlike and exploring activities of Vikings were at its peak. They intensified raids and cultural exchanges, and adopted a good part of the cultures with which they got in touch.

Kings of the Sea

Tightly linked to the sea, Vikings soon developed the liking for travelling and for maritime explorations, either with a commercial interest (they sold animal furs in exchange for other goods), or to pillage new territories. This is why they were able to reach the most diverse regions: on the east the borders of current Russia, in the center they reached Paris and looted the city; but without any doubt, their biggest accomplishment was in the west, when they established the first European settlement in North America, in Terranova Island.

SAILS
Later, Viking ships incorporated a keel in the hull, and a mast with a square sail.

Sailing

Vikings were the best ship builders of the time. The main Viking ship was the drakkar. Built with very strong wood, this oar ship was very light. There were also more robust versions of the drakkar, like the Knarr, designed for transportation and colonization.

Viking fleet. Illustration from the 19th century.

Sword in hand. Explorer Erik the Red in combat.

With a Proper Name

There were many the Viking adventurers who entered history for their explorations, discoveries and other deeds. These are only a few of the most notable ones:

Rurik
Scandinavian group native from the current Sweden and Denmark, lead by Riurik or Rurik (830-879), it explored the area of Lake Ladoga (Between Russia and Finland) in the year 862. In that pace they built the settlement of Holmgard, in Nóvgorod.

Ingolfur Arnarson
Arnarson was the first Viking settler in Iceland, where he arrived in 874. The legend says that, when he got close to unknown land, he ordered to throw the mast of the ship to the sea, and to disembark where it would touch land. That is how Reykjavik was founded.

Erik the red
Pirate, trader and explorer, in 981 he was sent into exile from Iceland. He travelled through the western coast of Greenland and after returning to his country, he convinced some people to settle there. His expedition departed in 985 with 25 ships; only 14 arrived.

GREAT BLACKSMITHS
Vikings owned an undisputable excellency in the forging of swords, knives and axes. On the left, handles of Viking swords.

Pioneer

Native from Iceland and second son of Erik the Red, Leif Eriksson (970-1020) is the most notable Viking explorer: it was him who colonized a small territory in North America five centuries before the arrival of Spaniards to the continent. His brother Thorvald used to travel with him, who was the first European who got in contact with the American Indians, and ended up dead in a fight against them.

First settlement. Ruins of the camp built by Vikings in the 10th century.

Feet in America

The settlement founded by Leif Eriksson was called Leifbundir and was located in the northern edge of Terranova Island. After a few decades it was definitely abandoned. It seems that constant attacks by local Indians were decisive for the Vikings to end the experience.

Leif Eriksson. Statue of the explorer in en Reykjavik (Iceland).

COINCIDENCE
The legend says that, after being appointed knight by King Olaf I of Norway, Leif got lost on his way back to Iceland, and arrived to North America by chance.

The Byzantine Empire

After the Roman Empire was divided in two parts, Western and Eastern, political importance was moved to the east of the Mediterranean. A new Civilization was being born around Constantinople, the Byzantine Empire, which would endure for all the European Middle Age.

Changes in the Mediterranean

Appearing in the year 395, the Eastern Roman Empire would soon leave behind its twin State in the West, immersed in a progressive decline. Constantinople, meeting place of the East and the Mare Nostrum, showed itself as the new economic and cultural center, with very particular religion and artistic sensitivity.

Constantinople. It joined two continents and three seas: it was destined to be a great metropolis.

The Byzantine Architectural Jewel

The Byzantine Empire reached its peak during the reign of Justinian (527-565). Aware that religion would help him to homogenize the different cultures under his ruling, the great Byzantine emperor invested in the construction of numerous temples and churches. Among them, the Basilica of Hagia Sophia. Jewel of architecture in Byzantium, it would become a mosque after the Ottoman conquest of the city in 1453.

The Long Agony of Decline

After emperor Justinian's death in 565, the secessionist tendency in the Byzantine colonies was increased. The territorial expanse of the Empire, its ethnic and religious diversity, and the expansion of Islam made survival more difficult. The confrontation between local aristocrats and the centralist power of Constantinople would, in time, cause the breaking apart.

SOLIDUS
Byzantine coin of the 6th century, with the image of emperor Justinian on one of its faces.

Byzantine art.
Eastern Christianity incorporated mosaic work and painting (icons) on the walls.

The Religious Schism

Religion was not able to keep out of the Roman Empire division. Far from Rome, the Eastern Church acquired its own profile. The serious discrepancies between them, which could not be fixed by councils or synods, ended in papal authority's rejection from Eastern Christianity and its final schism in 1504.

The Court of Byzantium

Even though the emperor (*basileus*) was the center of power, he covered a network of strong interests and changing alliances that wove in the court around the King. Any decompensation could lead to severe crisis.

Hidden Aspects of Power

The high clergy, high commands in the army, big traders and land owners were the sectors that encouraged the court. That was where political measures, large businesses, military campaigns and also theological roads were decided. Just like in other courts, when a crisis arose in the Empire, it was solved in an expedite manner: either by war, planned murder or conspiracy.

JUSTINIAN
Defender of Christianity, he entered history for his legal reform and for his expansion of the empire.

BELISARIUS
Military craftsman of the conquest of Ravenna, Belisarius stands to the right of the emperor, next to another Byzantine general.

THE EMPEROR
Justinian I the Great has a halo that highlights the divine condition of his position. He is holding a gold container as an offering.

THE BISHOP
The closeness of Maximiano of Ravenna with the emperor talks about the power of clergy and its support for Justinian. He is shown with three subordinates at his sides.

Byzantine Arguments

Byzantium was characterized for a bigger religious tolerance compared to the Roman Church. Its court was stage of long theological arguments whose written testimonies are a passionate tale of "Byzantine arguments" referring to endless and not very useful arguments.

THE CHI RHO
Adopted by Constantine as official symbol of the Roman Empire, this symbol that appears in the San Vital mosaic is formed by the initials of Christ's name in Greek: X and P.

THEODORA
She was despised by aristocracy for her humble origin. However, her influence over Justinian was very big.

Basilica of San Vitale

One of the most important temples of Byzantine art, the Basilica of San Vitale in Ravenna, was built by order of emperor Justinian from previous constructions. In its mosaics (especially the one presided by Justinian and Theodora) the main characters of the court are shown.

Outside. View of the Byzantine church of San Vitale.

SINGULARITIES
Byzantine mosaics are characterized for the lack of perspective, the use of gold in the backgrounds and their solemnity, in this case broken by the eunuch that opens the curtain.

THE EMPRESS
Just like Justinian, she has a halo that equals her to the emperor. To her solemn look, the luxury of her headdress and her tunic is added.

MOSAIC OF SAN VITALE
Presided by Justinian and Theodora, it is the most famous mosaic of the Basilica of San Vitale.

The Crusades

The Crusades were a series of military campaigns driven between the 11th and 13th centuries by Christians against the advance of Seljuk Turks and the Saracens. The excuse was to recover the Holy Land, considered an exclusive territory of Christianity.

The Holy War

During the reign of emperor Alexios I Komnenos (1081-1118), Byzantines managed to recover some of the territories lost to Seljuk Turks, but even so, Muslim armies were very near Constantinople. Also, in 1070, Jerusalem had fallen into Turk hands. Given the situation, Alexios I asked for help to Pope Urban II, who called the noblemen and kings of the West to war in favor of the Christians of the East. That is how the first of eight Crusades was born. They took place between the 11th and 13th centuries in Near East.

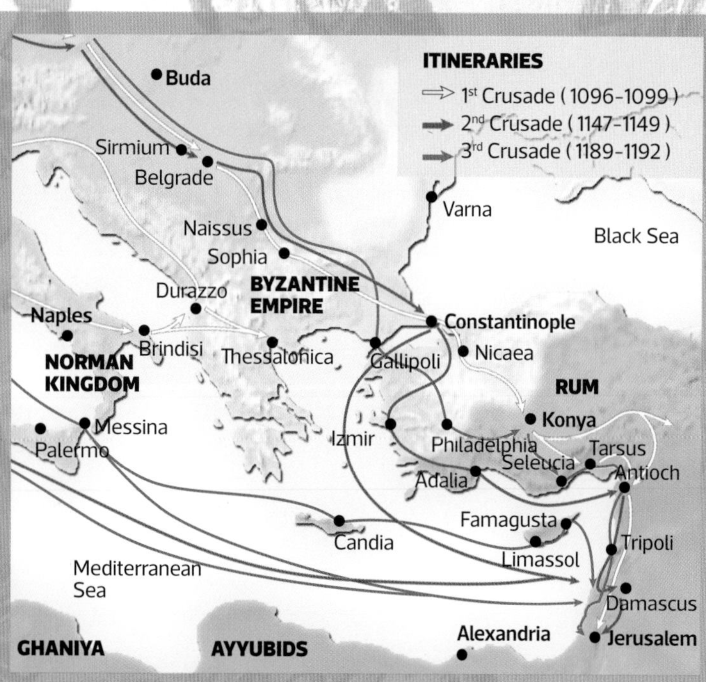

Strategic Objectives

While Alexios I was suspicious about the papal offering but accepted it with conditions, the church in Rome took advantage of the situation to act as one more kingdom of the many in which the Western Roman Empire had been divided. And as such, beyond religious motivation, it planned to control a strategic passage for Mediterranean trade with Asia. However, the conquered territories finally stayed in the hands of Byzantium.

HOSPITALLERS
In order to protect the pilgrims to the Holy Land, religious orders were created that later changed into military, like the one of the Hospitallers, born in 1084.

TEMPLARS
This order was born near the Temple of Jerusalem in 1119. It accumulated great wealth until it was accused of heresy and suppressed in 1312.

TEUTONIC KNIGHTS
Founded in 1189 by German knights, the Teutonic Order ruled over Lithuania, Prussia, Estonia and Poland until 1466.

Main Crusades

1 The First Crusade
Around 35,000 men, divided in four contingents, arrived to Constantinople between 1096 and 1097. They swore loyalty to Alexios I and to hand over to Byzantium the territories they would recover from the Turks, in exchange for supplies. The crusaders conquered Jerusalem in 1099.

2 The Second Crusade
It was summoned by the Pope in 1145 after the fall of Edessa, the first crusader principality created in 1098. Several European kingdoms participated in it. It was a catastrophe and did not stop the Muslim advance.

3 The Third Crusade
Saladin (1138-1198) gathered Egypt and Syria under his command, conquering Jerusalem and the crusader kingdoms, except for some cities. A third crusade was summoned (1189), in which monarchs like Richard the Lionheart (in the image), king of England. There were still five more crusades.

The Islamic Empire

In the first third of the 7th century, in the heart of the Arabian Peninsula, a new religious, social and political system appeared, which in a little more than fifty years expanded from the Atlantic to India, and that we generally know as Islam.

The Caliphates

Arabs turned the extended controlled territory in a melting pot in which very diverse cultures were amalgamated, with a common language, Arab, and a creed, Islam. The new State had many political centers during the Middle Age, and went through moments of unity and of rupture, that did not distort its many contributions to Mankind. The Umayyad Caliphate (661-750), with capital in Damascus, and the Abbasid Caliphate (750-1258), which moved the center to Baghdad, were their most important historical stages.

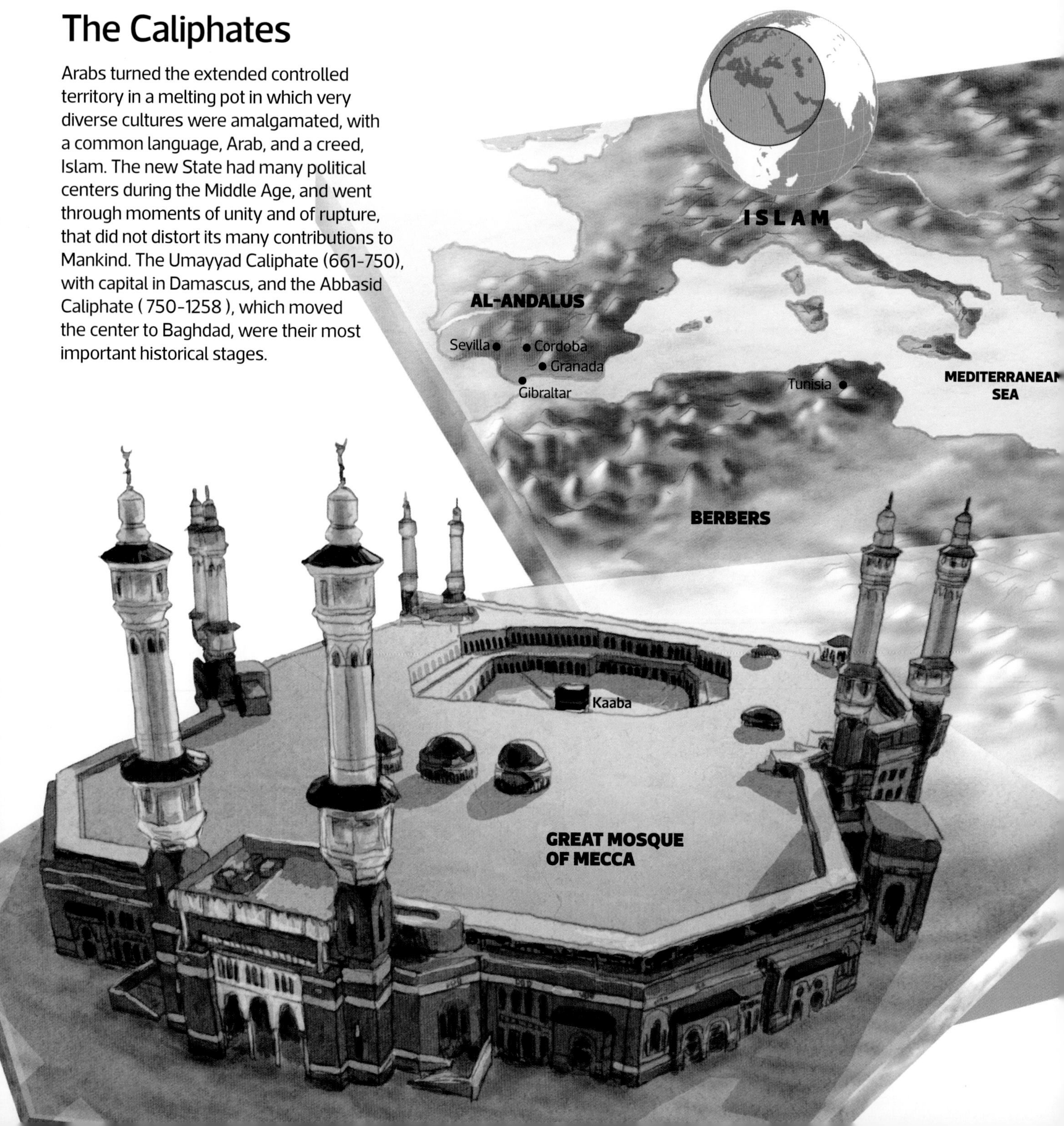

TRADE
Islam sent ivory and coral to China, and metal handcrafts to Europe. From Far East it imported silk fabrics and pottery. In the image, a jewelry box from the 10th century made in Herat.

Religion

The initiator of Islam was prophet Muhammad (c. 570-632). Islam established a religious body that participated in all aspects of private and public life of the faithful. Its sacred text is the Koran, which contains the set of precepts that all good Muslims must follow. The Mecca is the main holy place of Islam, in which Great Mosque the Kaaba is worshiped.

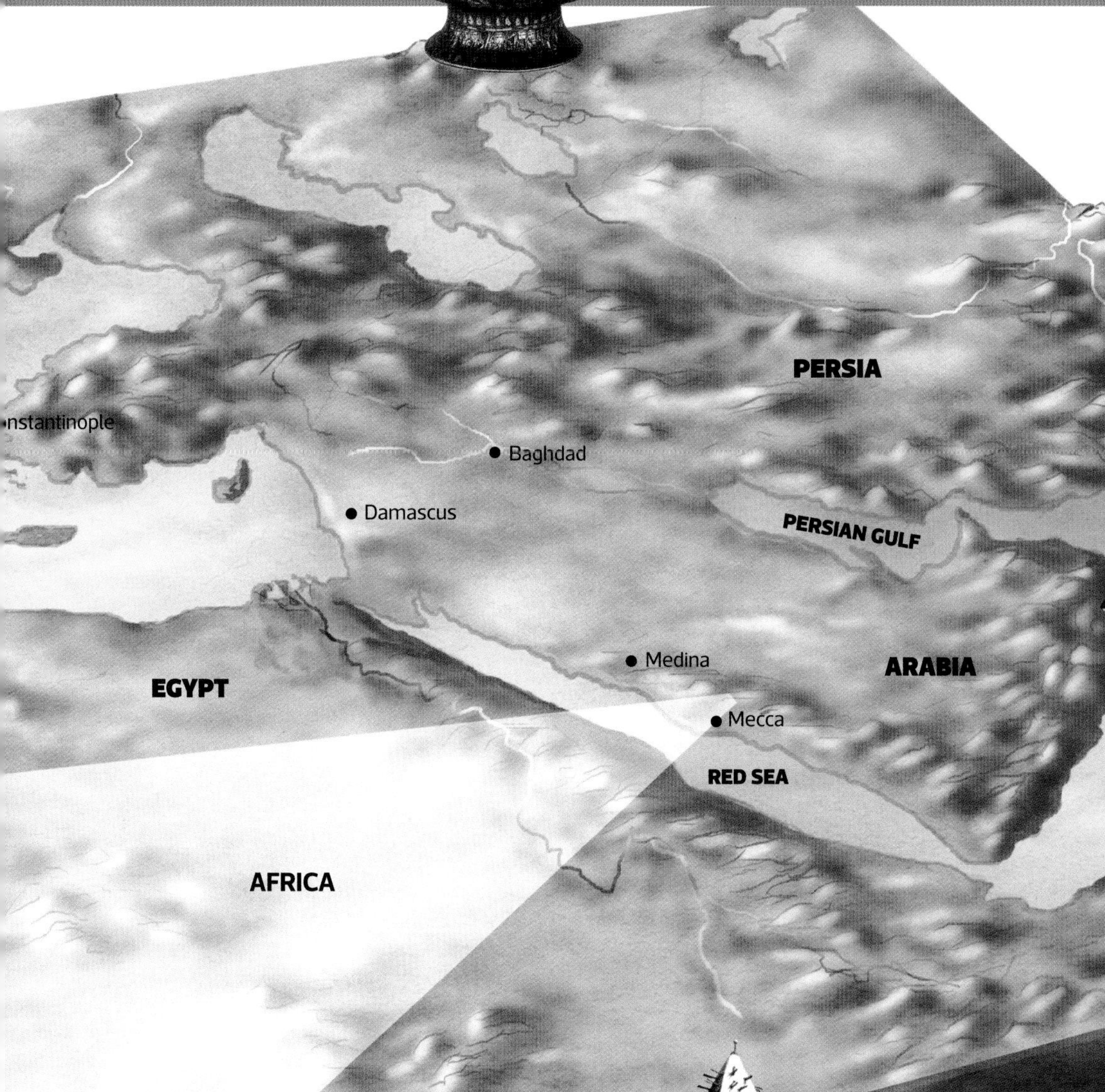

THE PROPHET
Angel Gabriel announced Muhammad his appointment as the last prophet, as this illustration shows.

Islamic miniature of the 8th century.

The Mosque

With its marked monumentality, this religious building is the biggest example of Islamic architectural creativity. Its slim towers (minarets) and large galleries, as well as the mihrab, a niche that indicates the direction of Mecca so the Muslim can point his prayers towards that place while praying, are characteristic of the mosque.

Diversity. Mosques like the Bobo Dioulasso, in Burkina Faso, show regional characteristics.

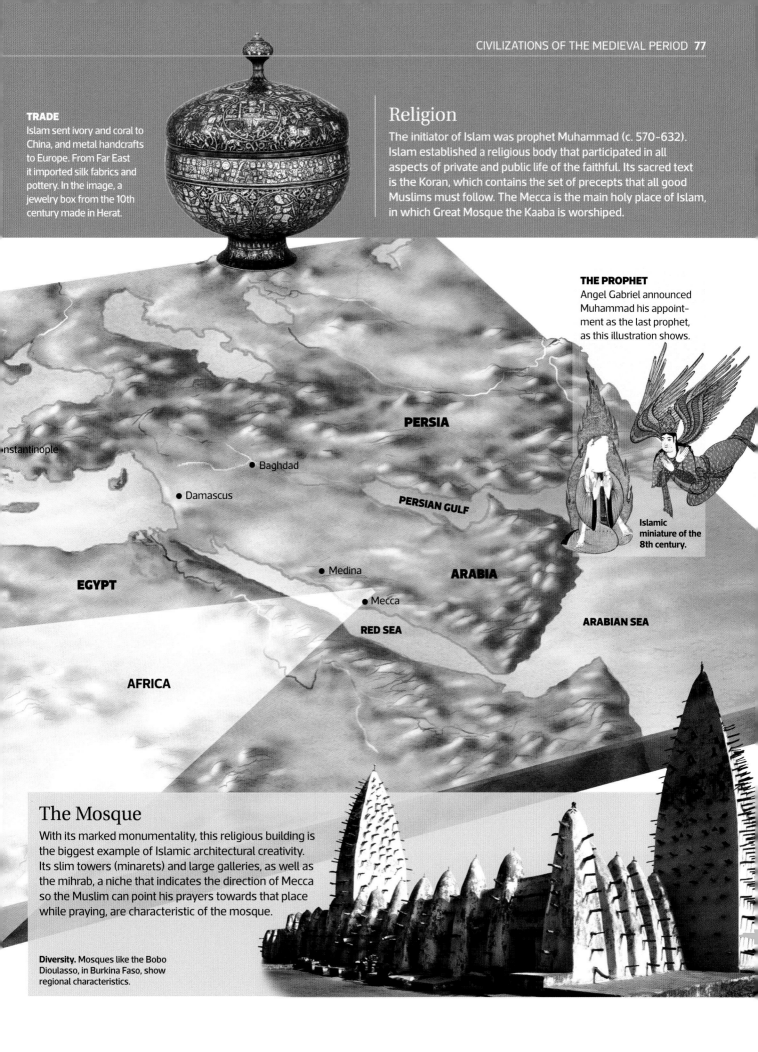

Baghdad, Abbasid Capital

Founded on the banks of the Tigris River by the Abbasid dynasty, it soon became the main city of the caliphate and underwent a major commercial, cultural and scientific development.

Life in the City

During the Islamic empire, Baghdad was surrounded by a double ring of protective walls, where there were four main gates. Inside, numerous stone buildings and decorated mosques were erected. The city was in constant turmoil, with its streets lined with artisans, vendors, buyers, readers of the Koran, students...

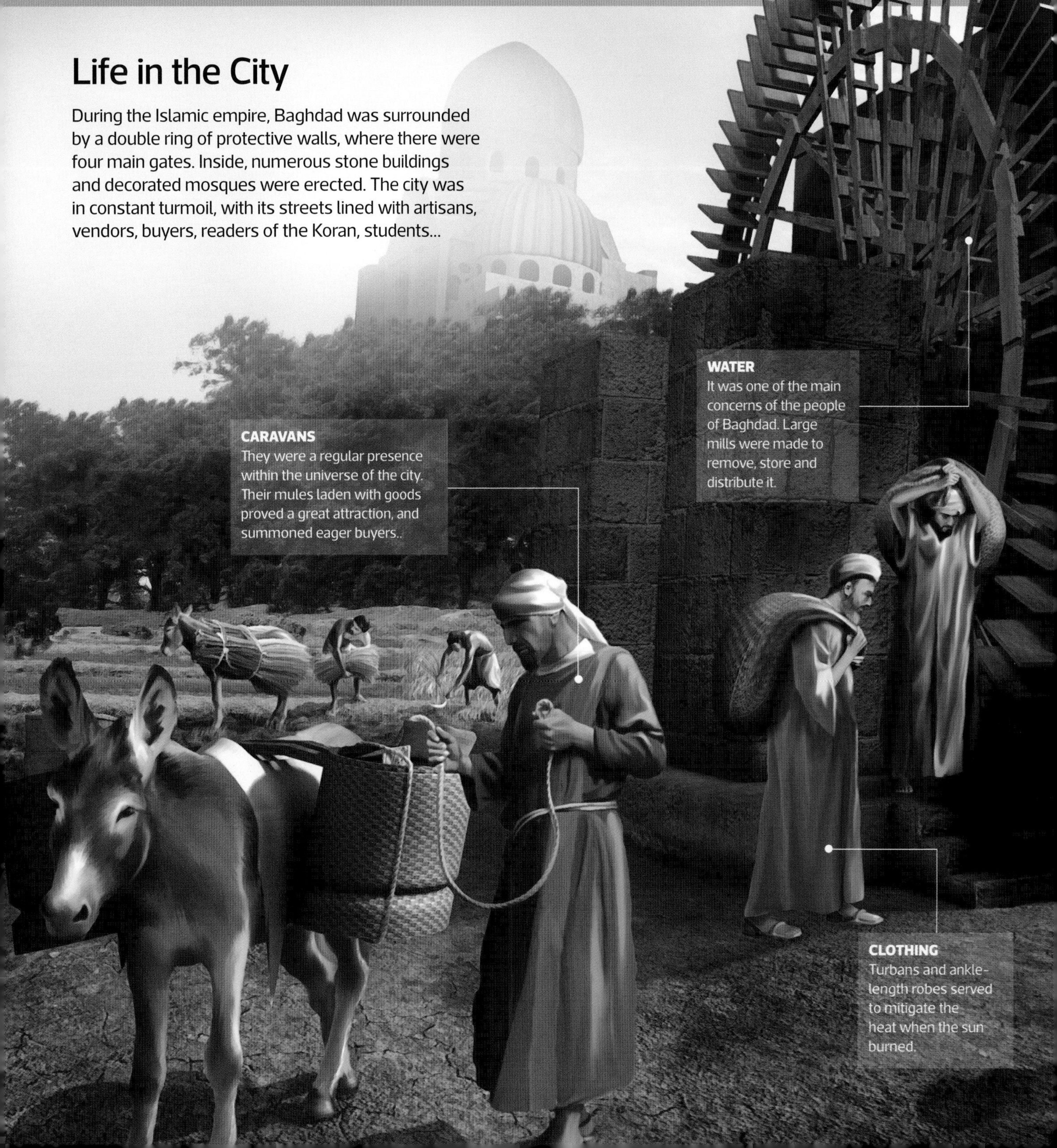

WATER
It was one of the main concerns of the people of Baghdad. Large mills were made to remove, store and distribute it.

CARAVANS
They were a regular presence within the universe of the city. Their mules laden with goods proved a great attraction, and summoned eager buyers..

CLOTHING
Turbans and ankle-length robes served to mitigate the heat when the sun burned.

A Great Capital

In 761, Caliph Al-Mansur founded Baghdad near the ruins of Babylon. Two centuries later, it had become one of the largest cities in the world. It had 700,000 inhabitants, almost as many as Constantinople.

READING
Learning the Koran was a sacred activity. In addition, the high scientific development encouraged intellectual exchange.

CHILDREN
The precepts and religious rites were the only skills required for children, there was no systematic schooling.

TEXTILES
Experts in manufacturing, vendors exhibited their garments, fabrics and carpets. Textiles were one of the most important manufactures.

ARTISANS
Among the artisans also highlighted glaziers, which produced vases, glasses and bottles.

The Maya and the Aztecs

Mesoamerica was in ancient times an important center of Civilization. Among the many cultures that flourished there include the Maya, who inhabited the Yucatan Peninsula, and the Aztecs, whose heyday took place later, in the valley of Mexico.

The Aztec Empire

Heirs of the Olmec, Zapotec, Toltec and Mixtec cultures, the Aztec rose in the 14th and 15th centuries as the Lords of the Valley of Mexico. From there they exercised their leadership until the arrival of the Spanish conquerors in 1521. In a very fast manner they went from being a tribal community to an independent State, strong and developed, whose capital, Tenochtitlan, would be the most spectacular of their testimonies.

Religion

Aztecs were pantheistic, worshiping various deities associated with nature and the cosmos: the sun, moon, fire, rain... They consecrated ceremonies including human sacrifices, the most valuable offering.

Quetzalcoatl. A very important Aztec deity.

XIUHTECUHTLI
Priests were consecrated to a numerous cast of deities, among them Xiuhtecuhtli (in the image), God of fire and daylight.

MASKS
Jade mask making is one of the greatest expressions of Aztec art.

Maya Splendor

The Classic Period, from mid-third century to the 11th century, is the one with greatest progress of Maya culture. It is the time of the great cities of the north, which experienced sustained population growth thanks to stability and prosperity. On the left, terracotta statuette of this period.

GULF DE MEXICO
La Venta
Comalcalco
Palenque
Tonini
Bonampak
Chinkultic
Nebaj
PETÉN
Quiringua
Copan
Tikal
Caracol
Lamanai
Edzna
Uxmal
Dzibilchaltun
Chichen Itza
Coba
Tulum
YUCATAN PENINSULA
PACIFIC OCEAN
CHICHEN ITZA

THE MAYA

THE PYRAMIDS
The Maya built these monuments following a four stepped faces model, usually crowned with a ritual temple.

The Maya

The Maya settled over a wide and rich territory, crossed by many rivers. In the valleys, they spread an efficient agriculture, basis of their survival. They also took advantage of the resources that the coast and extended central and western plains provided. They founded great city-states such as Tikal, Chichen Itza, Copan and Palenque, all of them centers of an exceptional development.

Sacred Stone

The Maya stood out for stone carving. Stelaes [like this one of Tikal (current Guatemala) from the 8th century], in which they carved commemorative images, are among the most notable examples.

Cultural Legacy in Mesoamerica

The two largest Civilizations of Mesoamerica had a great cultural and scientific development that still marvel the world. Architecture, painting, sculptures, calendars, numerical systems, glyphs... constitute the cultural heritage left behind by Mayas and Aztecs.

Near the Sky

Maya Civilization stood out for its extraordinary ability to build funeral monuments, urban houses, and royal palaces and, especially, pyramid temples, located in such a way to allow astronomical observation. The high altitude of the temples, around 40-50 m. looked for an approach to deities and stars, which they studied so much.

TOWER
In the Great Palace of Palenque its squared base tower stands out, uncommon in Mayan architecture.

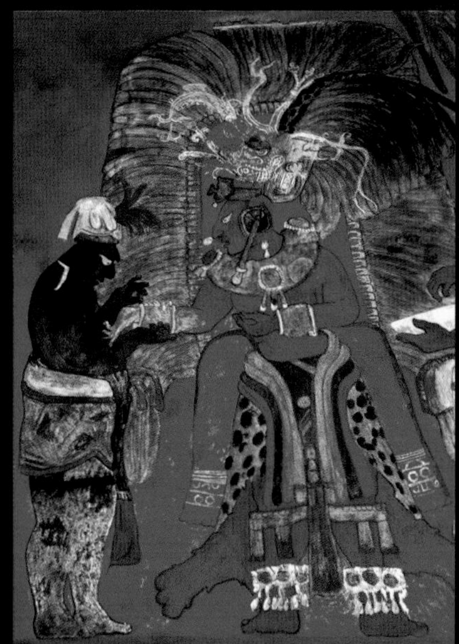

MURALS OF BONAMPAK
With an exceptional control of color, the Maya recreated the great milestones of their historical and economical development in decorative and funerary paintings.

Palenque

Although smaller tan Copan or Tikal, the Mayan city of Palenque, in the current Mexico, is famous for its great buildings and sculptures built between 226 BC and 1123. In the image, the Great Palace (to the left) and the Temple of Inscriptions.

SCIENCE
The Maya invented a numerical system that included the zero. In astronomy, they created two kinds of calendars. To the left, a commemorative vase.

GLYPHS
The Temple of Inscriptions owes its name to the planks with glyphs that explain the history of the leading clan of the city.

Aztec Codices

These documents revealed the essential characteristics of Aztec society and their advances. Made as pictographic manuscripts, most of them combined drawing with text in Nahuatl language. They are classified in prehispanic and colonial. The first ones were made on fig tree or maguey paper, deer skin or cotton fabric; the latter, in European paper, industrial fabric and parchment.

Mendoza Codex. Made around 1542. In its 71 pages they talk about kings and Aztec conquests.

Quetzal

Eagle

Hummingbird

Parrot

Aztec Sculpture

In Aztec art, what stands out are the Stone carvings. The great sculptures usually represented deities and kings, and were exhibited in temples. Due to their symbolism, they communicated religious events and were used during some rituals. The smaller ones usually represented animals and common objects.

Coatlicue. Statue of the Goddess of Earth, preserved in the National Museum of Mexico.

The Incas

On the basis of the cultural experience of the Central Andes (civilization center since the third millennium BC), the Incas consolidated a powerful and expansionist empire, Tawantinsuyu, along the Andes range in the 15th and 16th centuries.

Organization

The Incas, builders of aqueducts and canals and a system of agricultural terraces that allowed them to grow crops on the slopes of the mountains, based their great development, expansion and progress on an excellent social and political organisation. This allowed them to articulate a vast territory and to maintain their supremacy in the Andes. The ruler of the Empire, the Inca, was considered a sacred being: the son of the Sun. In addition, he headed the elite hierarchy of Cusco, the capital.

Life after Death

The religious conception of Andean societies included the concept of the afterlife. There was a heavenly kingdom for the virtuous and noble, and sinners would go to a kind of hell where they were hungry and cold.

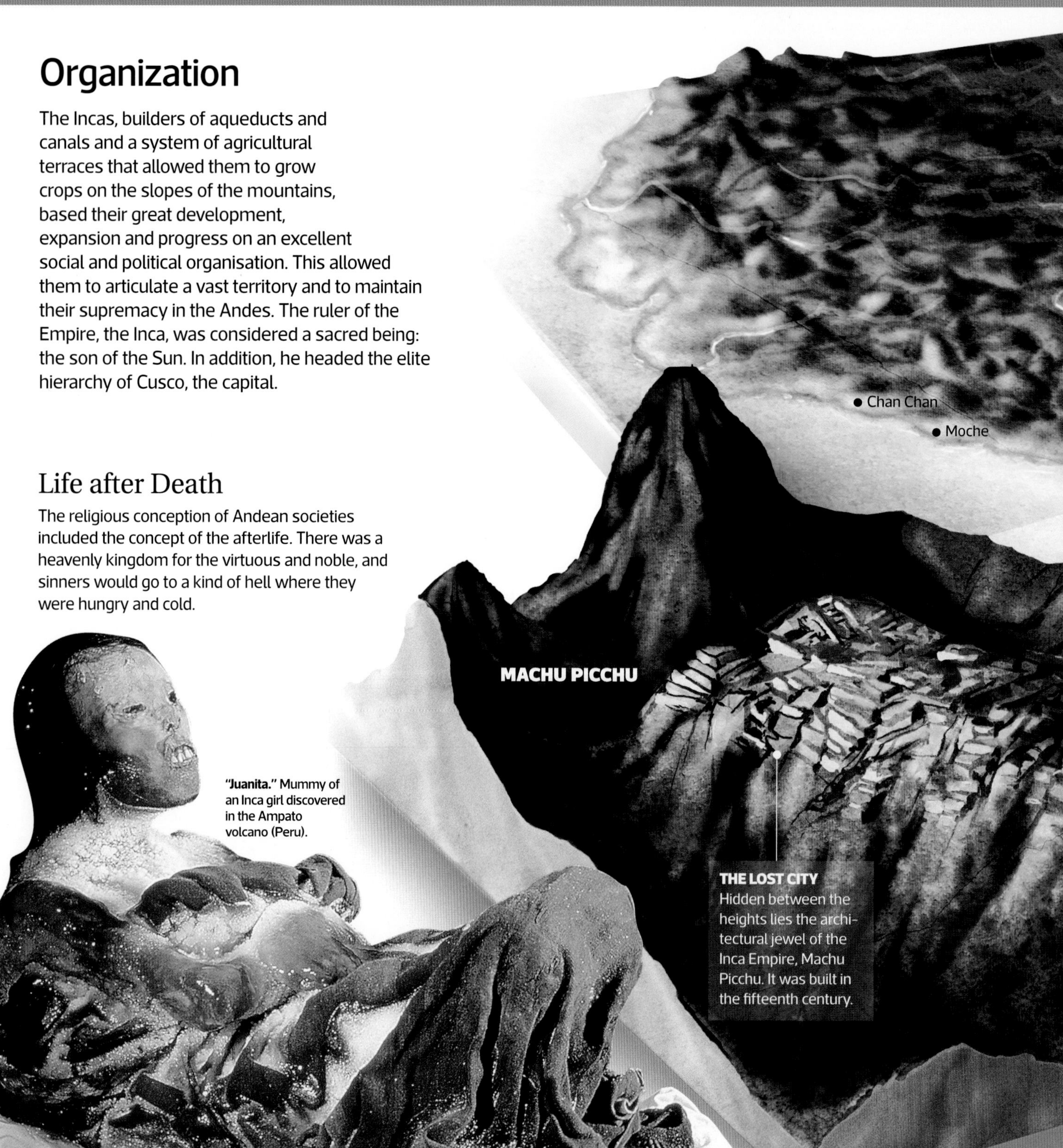

"Juanita." Mummy of an Inca girl discovered in the Ampato volcano (Peru).

THE LOST CITY
Hidden between the heights lies the architectural jewel of the Inca Empire, Machu Picchu. It was built in the fifteenth century.

High-Quality Agriculture

The development achieved by previous Andean societies and the Inca Empire was sustained by its agricultural productivity. They dominated the planting, harvesting and irrigation techniques, and were skilful administrators of agricultural surpluses.

Peasants. The Incas cultivated mainly maize, potatoes and beans. The picture is a drawing by chronicler Guaman Poma de Ayala.

The Tawantinsuyu

In 1400, the Incas dominated the valley of Cusco. From then onwards, the rapidly expanded their borders, reaching part of Ecuador and Colombia, on the north, and part of Argentina and Chile towards the south.

Ritual Cultures

The organisation of worship and ritual practices were at the heart of the Inca religion. At the top of the divine pantheon, Viracocha, the "Lord and Master of the World," was supported by a large cast of gods among which there was Inti, the Sun. In the picture, an Inca ceremonial glass.

The Inca Road Network

One of the main strengths of Tawantinsuyu was the ability to maintain communication between Cusco and the rest of the Empire, thanks to a remarkably effective system of roads, stops and messaging.

A Centralized State

The land communication network of the Inca Empire allowed its leaders to exercise an administrative centralisation and the control of the entire territory that still amazes specialists. The messengers or chaskis covered over two hundred kilometers a day through these ways, among which, the 2.400-km-long Camino Real, linking Cusco and Quito, is highlighted.

ROADS
In general, they followed a straight line of assembled rocks. They crossed mountains, jungles and streams, in the middle of the Andes.

WATCHERS
From above, the messengers were distinguished by a white feather headdress that identified them.

ROTATION
A chaski awaited the arrival of the bearer of the message. He could walk more than 240 km in one day.

SPEED
The chaskis were recruited among the youngest ones to take advantage of their speed.

FOOD
Some stops along the way had corrals with llamas and small gardens to meet the needs of the messengers.

THE STOPS
They were shelters for the runners to rest. The most equipped ones had rooms.

Traveling

In addition to serving the chaskis, the network of Inca roads also facilitated the movement of military contingents of Tawantinsuyu, both for conquest and for the defence of the vast Inca territory. At some points of the network, the state built large stone forts, usually walled.

Ollataytambo.
Ruins of the fortress of this Inca city close to Cusco.

THE QUIPU
Depending on the complexity of the message, it could be memorized or registered in a quipu, the Incan numerical notation system based on knotted cords.

Imperial Japan

The insularity of Japan, a small country fragmented into thousands of islands, has been instrumental in its history. The power key always belonged to the person who owned and controlled the land, which caused centuries of feudal clashes.

The Feudal Era

During the Middle Ages, Japan went through a slow but profound change from a highly centralised monarchy to a complex feudal system. The Yamato Empire, in the Kofun period (300-710) was the initiator of a political tradition on the island. During the Heian period (8th to 12th century), with the family clan system already settled, the Fujiwara Dynasty ruled. The power struggles between clans marked the Japanese medieval history.

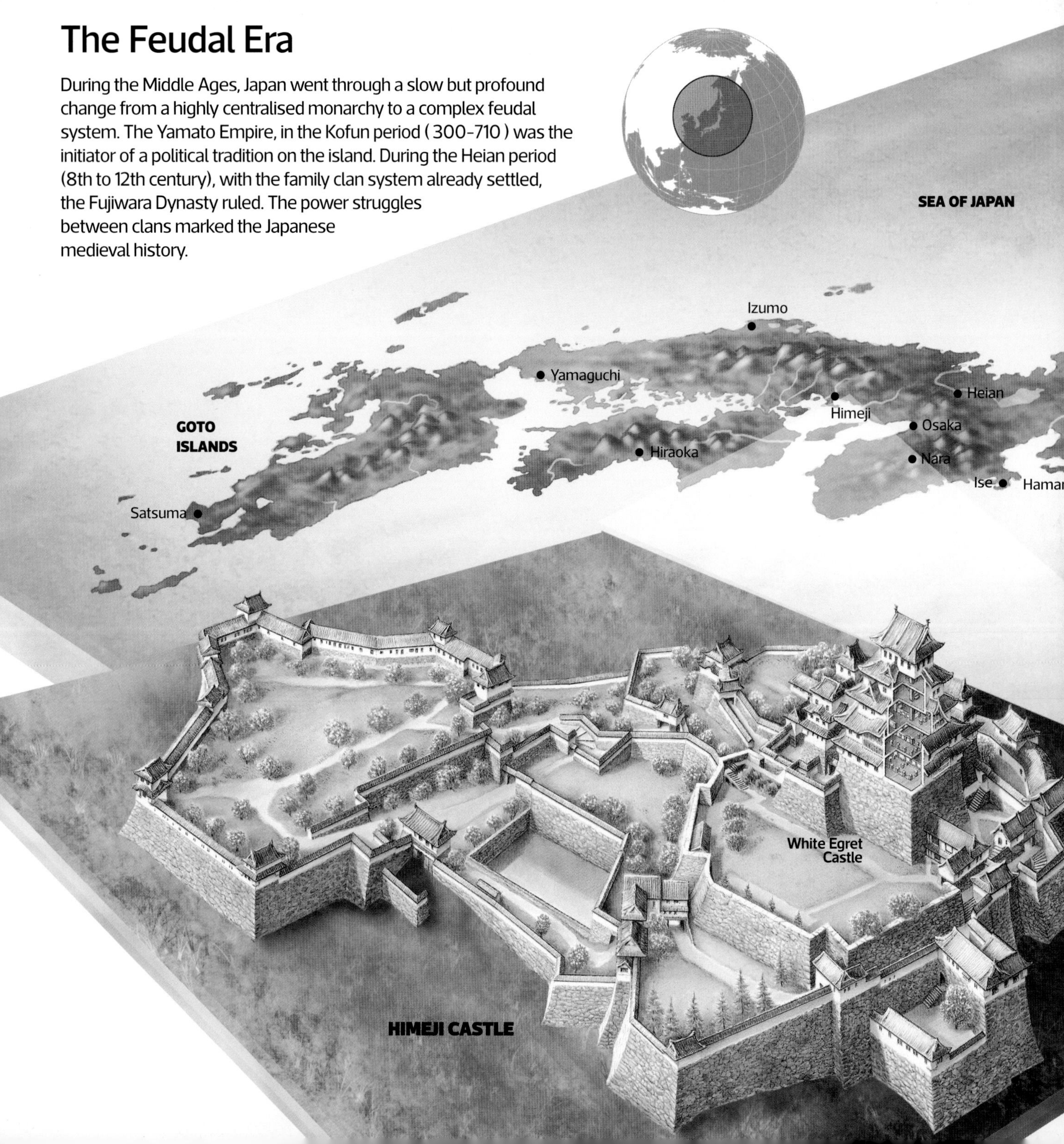

THE SAMURAI
The samurai warrior figure is closely linked to medieval Japan. Miyamoto Musashi (see image) was a famous 18th century samurai.

Religion

There are three different main branches within the belief system of Japan: popular mythology, Shinto and Buddhism. Over the centuries, they started to criss-cross in the religious syncretism that characterizes Japanese culture. Confucianism has also been influential, especially in the Tokugawa era.

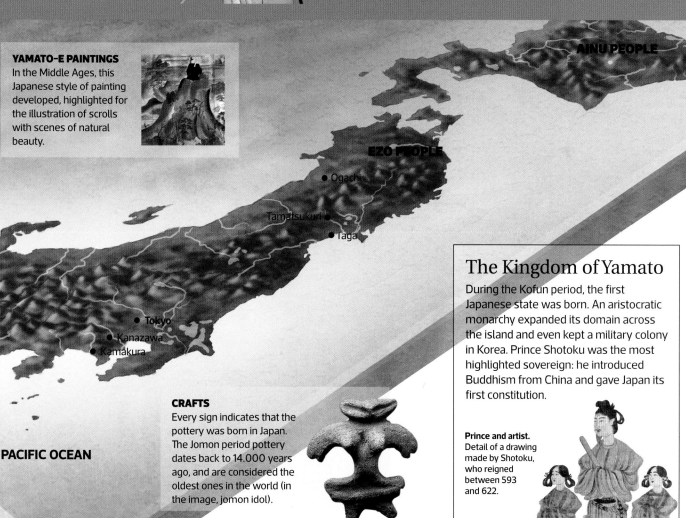

YAMATO-E PAINTINGS
In the Middle Ages, this Japanese style of painting developed, highlighted for the illustration of scrolls with scenes of natural beauty.

AINU PEOPLE

EZO PEOPLE

Ogachi

Tamatsukuri

Taga

Tokyo

Kanazawa

Kamakura

PACIFIC OCEAN

CRAFTS
Every sign indicates that the pottery was born in Japan. The Jomon period pottery dates back to 14.000 years ago, and are considered the oldest ones in the world (in the image, jomon idol).

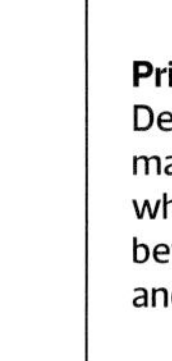

The Kingdom of Yamato

During the Kofun period, the first Japanese state was born. An aristocratic monarchy expanded its domain across the island and even kept a military colony in Korea. Prince Shotoku was the most highlighted sovereign: he introduced Buddhism from China and gave Japan its first constitution.

Prince and artist. Detail of a drawing made by Shotoku, who reigned between 593 and 622.

The Pagoda

With its tiered roofs, the pagoda is one of the main buildings of traditional Japanese architecture and other Asian countries such as China and Thailand. It is an evolution of the Indian stupa. A good example of this type of building, usually of religious nature, are the Golden Temple in Kyoto (see picture) and the With Egret Temple, within the majestic feudal castle of Himeji (see drawing).

Japanese Clans

Composed by a family group that shared the same ancestors, the clan always had a military leader in charge of the defence of the people. Over time, the clans ended up running the country, marginalizing the emperor.

Fujiwara Hegemony

Over the 5th to 8th century, a system of family clans was consolidated in Japan, which came to adopt an administrative bureaucracy and a military force of their own. With the transfer of the capital to Heian in 794, the Heian period began, marked by the dominance of the Fujiwara clan, which tried to centralize the country. The aim of centralisation of the new administration was limited and, gradually, various military clans accumulated power in the provinces. Until the 19th century, clans alternated in power.

Byōdō-in. Buddhist temple completed in 1053, during the Heian period in Uji, Kyoto.

The New capital

The city of Heian (Tokyo) was characterized during the rule of the Fujiwara by an idle ruling class surrounded by luxuries, a model far from the Chinese administrative efficiency that was the basis for the hegemony of Chang'an during the government of the Han Dynasty.

The Heian Period

During part of this period, the Fujiwara clan concentrated almost absolute power due to of its ties to the imperial house, the monopoly of major political positions and the possession of large pieces of land. After a period of conflict, in the twelfth century, the Minamoto family managed to overtake supremacy in 1192.

ROYAL GUARDIAN
Figure of a soldier of the Fujiwara period, showing the typical dress of the military.

Minamoto no Yoritomo. 12th century portrait of the first Minamoto shogun.

Fujiwara no Michinaga

His mandate marked the pinnacle of the Fujiwara power. In 995, after being appointed chief advisor to the Emperor, he ignored the central administration and ruled from his private chancellery.

The Minamoto Clan

After the victory of the Minamoto clan, a military government was established, the Kamukara shogunate (1192-1333), which gave power to warrior classes. The Minamoto family concentrated all the power in the country. The founder of the clan was Minamoto no Yoritomo, proclaimed shogun in 1192.

Tokugawa Ieyasu. Founder of the Tokugawa shogunate (also called Edo) in the 17th century.

NOH THEATRE
Official entertainment for the military aristocracy during the Edo period, the origins of this drama style date back to a rural show of the 13th century.

The Shogunates

Between the 12th and 19th centuries, the classical period of Japanese feudalism developed. The shogun (army commander, a title given by the emperor) emerged as the *de facto* ruler of the country, although officially the function fell on the emperor. Shoguns came to control all political, military and diplomatic decisions of the State. The three main Japanese shogunates were the Kamakura (dominated by Minamoto and Hojo clans), the Ashikaga and the Tokugawa.

Chronology

In the history of Japan, several fundamental periods can be distinguished, especially marked by struggles between the different family clans with more power in the Empire.

794-1192
Heian
Dominated by the Fujiwara clan, which urged centralisation and promoted a court culture.

1192-1333
Kamakura
First feudal regime initiated by the Minamoto clan, and continued by Hojo. Period of mongol invasions.

1336-1573
Ashikaga
Second shogunate, full of instability and succession struggles. Repression of peasants and Christians.

1604-1867
Tokugawa
Strengthening of the shogunate and expansion of feudalism. Isolationism was imposed in the country.

1868-1912
Meiji
Major political, economic and cultural reforms. End of feudalism and of the shogunate power.

Glossary

ALLUVIAL Relating to or derived from alluvium, or a deposit of clay, silt, sand, and gravel left by flowing streams in a river valley or delta, typically producing fertile soil.

ANNEX A building joined with a main building.

ARCHAIC From an early period of art or culture.

DESPOTIC Typical of a despot, or someone who is tyrannical.

DIASPORA The dispersion of a people from their homeland.

FRAGMENTATION Breaking or being broken into small or separate parts.

FRIEZE A broad horizontal band of sculpted or painted decoration, especially on a wall near the ceiling.

HIERARCHY A system in which people or groups are ranked according to status or authority.

HIEROGLYPH A stylized picture of an object representing a word, syllable, or sound.

IDEOGRAM A written character symbolizing the idea of a thing without indicating the sounds used to say it.

INAUGURATE To introduce a system, policy, or period.

INCARNATION A person who embodies in the flesh a deity, spirit, or abstract quality.

INTERLOCUTOR A person who takes part in a dialogue.

MANIFESTATION An action that embodies something, especially a theory or an abstract idea.

METALLURGY The science concerned with the properties of metals and their production and purification.

MOSQUE A Muslim place of worship.

NECROPOLIS A large cemetery belonging to an ancient city.

NEOLITHIC Relating to the later part of the Stone Age.

OLIGARCHY A small group of people who have control of a country.

PAPYRUS A material prepared in ancient Egypt for writing or painting on and also for making rope, sandals, and boats.

PATRIARCHAL A system of society or government controlled by men.

PATRICIAN Characteristic of the aristocracy.

PHARAOH An ancient Egyptian ruler.

PHONEME Any of the perceptually distinct units of sound in a specified language that distinguish one word from another.

PHONOGRAM A symbol representing a sound.

PLEBEIAN A commoner of ancient Rome.

POLEIS A city-state in ancient Greece.

PRIMITIVE A person belonging to a relatively unadvanced society or culture.

PROHIBITION The act of forbidding something, especially by law.

SCRIBE A person who copies out documents.

STYLUS An ancient writing implement.

TERRA-COTTA Unglazed earthenware used as ornamental building material or in modeling.

For More Information

Archaeological Institute of America Headquarters

Boston University

656 Beacon Street, 6th Floor

Boston, MA 02215-2006

(617) 353-9361

Website: http://www.archaeological.org

The Archaeological Institute of America (AIA) is a not-for-profit group founded in 1879. It is North America's oldest and largest organization devoted to the world of archaeology.

Canadian Archaeological Association

Indigenous Studies and History

Brantford Campus

Wilfrid Laurier University

73 George St.

Brantford, ON N3T 2Y3

Website: http://www.canadianarchaeology.com

Founded in 1968, the Canadian Archaeological Association (CAA) invites professional, avocational, and student archaeologists.

Metropolitan Museum of Art

1000 Fifth Avenue

New York, NY 10028

(212) 535-7710

Website: http://www.metmuseum.org

The Metropolitan Museum of Art showcases more than 5,000 years of art from around the world and from all civilizations.

Society for Historical Archaeology

13017 Wisteria Drive #395

Germantown, MD 20874

(301) 972-9684

Website: http://www.sha.org

Formed in 1967, the Society for Historical Archaeology (SHA) is the largest scholarly group concerned with the archaeology of the modern world (1400–present) and promotes scholarly research and the dissemination of knowledge concerning historical archaeology.

WEBSITES

Because of the changing nature of internet links, Rosen Publishing has developed an online list of websites related to the subject of this book. This site is updated regularly. Please use this link to access the list:

http://www.rosenlinks.com/VHW/civilizations

For Further Reading

Brier, Bob. *The Secret of the Great Pyramid: How One Man's Obsession Led to the Solution of Ancient Egypt's Greatest Mystery.* Washington, DC: Smithsonian Books, 2008.

Carlsen, William. *Jungle of Stone: The True Story of Two Men, Their Extraordinary Journey, and the Discovery of the Lost Civilization of the Maya.* New York, NY: William Morrow, 2016.

Catling, Christopher. *A Practical Handbook of Archaeology: A Beginner's Guide to Unearthing the Past.* London, England: Hermes House, 2014.

Connelly, Joan B. *The Parthenon Enigma.* New York, NY: Alfred A. Knopf, 2014.

Dalley, Stephanie. *Myths from Mesopotamia: Creation, the Flood, Gilgamesh, and Others.* New York, NY: Oxford University Press, 2000.

Kriwaczek, Paul. *Babylon: Mesopotamia and the Birth of Civilization.* New York, NY: Thomas Dunne Books, 2012.

Lassieur, Allison. *Ancient Mesopotamia.* New York, NY: Children's Press, 2012.

Mertz, Barbara. *Temples, Tombs & Hieroglyphs: A Popular History of Ancient Egypt.* New York, NY: Harper, 2009.

Parpola, Asko. *The Roots of Hinduism: The Early Aryans and the Indus Civilization.* New York, NY: Oxford University Press, 2015.

Williams, Marcia. *Ancient Egypt: Tales of Gods and Pharaohs.* Somerville, MA: Candlewick Press, 2011.

Wright, David P. *Inventing God's Law: How the Covenant Code of the Bible Used and Revised the Laws of Hammurabi.* New York, NY: Oxford University Press, 2009.

Index